MUSSAURUS

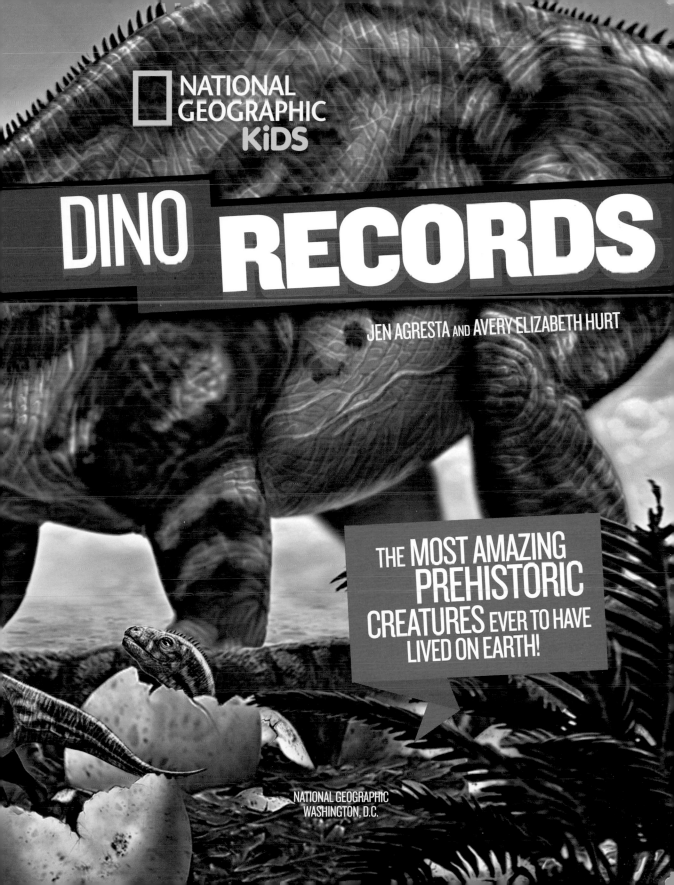

NATIONAL GEOGRAPHIC KiDS

DINO RECORDS

JEN AGRESTA AND AVERY ELIZABETH HURT

THE MOST AMAZING PREHISTORIC CREATURES EVER TO HAVE LIVED ON EARTH!

NATIONAL GEOGRAPHIC
WASHINGTON, D.C.

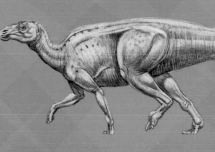

CHAPTER 5: **MOST INTRIGUING** 122

CHAPTER 6: **FIRST** 150

CHAPTER 7: **PREHISTORIC ANIMALS** 178

ARE YOU READY TO TRAVEL BACK IN TIME?

GET READY FOR AN ADVENTURE OF PREHISTORIC PROPORTIONS.

You probably already know that dinosaurs are some of the biggest, most diverse, and coolest-looking creatures ever to have inhabited the planet. But did you also know that dinos didn't start out that way? About 270 million years ago, our planet had just one giant landmass—called Pangaea—instead of the seven continents we have today. Over tens of millions of years, as the movement of Earth's tectonic plates broke up Pangaea into smaller pieces with different climates and landscapes, dinosaurs evolved into record-breaking species of all shapes and sizes— complete with the amazing armor, spikes, sails, horns, plates, frills, and other awesomely impressive attributes we recognize today in books, in movies, and lurking on toy store shelves.

In National Geographic Kids' *Dino Records* you'll meet not only the biggest, smallest, deadliest, and weirdest dinos, but also the winners for most famous, most peculiar posterior, and most magical name. You'll find fantastic firsts, from the first dinos on Earth to the first dinos in space. And you'll meet other rad record-breaking creatures that lived before, after, and alongside dinosaurs. Did you know that the largest sea turtle and the largest flying animal (both now extinct) shared the planet with dinosaurs? Distant relatives of crocs and sharks did, too, and some managed to survive the event that doomed the dinos. Mammals—no bigger than a dog when dinos roamed—eventually evolved after the extinction into massive creatures, including the biggest land mammal that ever lived. Turn the page to stomp, swim, and soar back in time!

THE AGE OF DINOSAURS!

Dinosaurs roamed the Earth during a time known as the Mesozoic era, which spanned approximately 251 to 65 million years ago (or "mya"). Scientists divide the Mesozoic era into three periods: the Triassic, the Jurassic, and the Cretaceous. Dinosaurs first appeared during the Triassic period, eventually becoming the dominant animals on land. Dinos ruled from the start of the Jurassic period until the mass extinction at the end of the Cretaceous period, which wiped out about three-quarters of the species on Earth.

ISANOSAURUS

TRIASSIC 251–200 MYA

First appearance of dinosaurs, pterosaurs, turtles, flies, bony fish, and mammals. Dinos included *Eoraptor*, *Herrerasaurus*, *Isanosaurus*, *Coelophysis*, and *Plateosaurus*.

STEGOSAURUS

JURASSIC
200–145 MYA

First appearance of salamanders, hermit crabs, true lizards, blood-sucking insects, and birds. Dinos included *Allosaurus*, *Compsognathus*, *Archaeopteryx*, *Brachiosaurus*, *Stegosaurus*, and *Diplodocus*.

CRETACEOUS
145–65 MYA

First appearance of flowering plants, bees, ants, snakes, and termites. Dinos included *Spinosaurus*, *Triceratops*, *Ankylosaurus*, *Corythosaurus*, *Microraptor*, *Argentinosaurus*, *Velociraptor*, *Maiasaura*, *Pachycephalosaurus*, *Troodon*, and *Tyrannosaurus*.

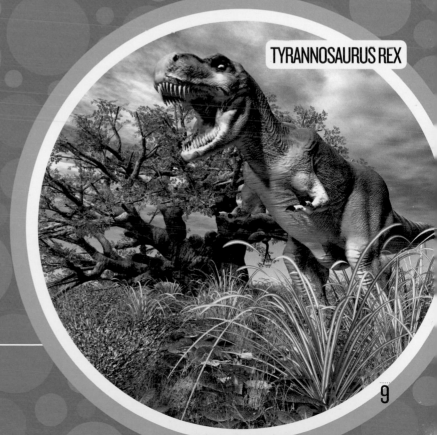

TYRANNOSAURUS REX

CHAPTER 1

MEET SOME OF THE BIGGEST ANIMALS EVER TO HAVE ROAMED THE EARTH!

Most people know that dinosaurs were big. But just how big did they get? Try this on for size: It would take you and more than 1,500 of your friends combined to reach the weight of the winner of this chapter! Turn the page (if you dare ...)

FUTALOGNKOSAURUS

BIGGEST 11

THE TITANOSAUR

(TIE-TAN-OH-SORE)

Titanosaurs were mega-colossal sauropod dinosaurs—long-necked plant-eaters whose ranks included the largest dinos that ever lived. In 2012 a rancher in a remote area of the Patagonia region of Argentina found a bone belonging to what scientists now believe may be the largest titanosaur of all ... and the biggest animal ever to have walked the Earth. More than 220 bones from this still-to-be-officially-named species (which is being called simply "the Titanosaur") have been excavated, allowing paleontologists to estimate the weight of this humongous herbivore at a whopping 70 tons (63.5 t)—about as much as 10 African elephants, the largest land animal alive today. The Titanosaur's neck alone was about as long as a school bus, and its heart—which may have weighed as much as three adult humans—could pump almost 24 gallons (90 L) of blood in one beat!

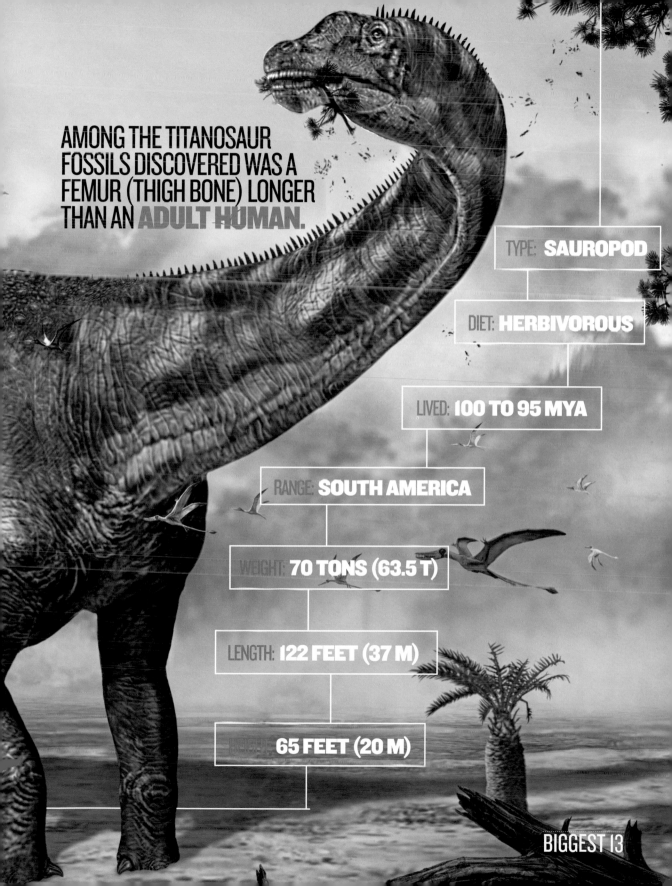

AMONG THE TITANOSAUR FOSSILS DISCOVERED WAS A FEMUR (THIGH BONE) LONGER THAN AN **ADULT HUMAN.**

TYPE: **SAUROPOD**

DIET: **HERBIVOROUS**

LIVED: **100 TO 95 MYA**

RANGE: **SOUTH AMERICA**

WEIGHT: **70 TONS (63.5 T)**

LENGTH: **122 FEET (37 M)**

HEIGHT: **65 FEET (20 M)**

BIGGEST 13

THE RUNNERS-UP ...

These spectacular sauropods marched into the record books as some of the biggest animals of all time.

ARGENTINOSAURUS

(AHR-GEN-TEEN-OH-SORE-US)

The name of this massive South American sauropod means "Argentina's lizard"; do you know where it was found? You guessed it: Argentina! Thought to have been longer than a professional basketball court and about as heavy as 70 bison, the herbivore would likely have had to eat 100,000 calories of vegetation per day to reach its adult size—about the equivalent of 1,000 bananas! Like our winner, *Argentinosaurus* was a titanosaur and may well have been as immense. But because estimates of its size are based on far fewer remains, the yet unnamed titanosaur takes our crown.

FUTALOGNKOSAURUS
(FOO-TA-LONG-KOH-SOR-US)

Stretching between 105 and 112 feet (32 and 34 m) long and standing as tall as a four-story building, *Futalognkosaurus dukei* roamed the late Cretaceous in an area that is now Argentina (which, as you may have begun to notice, is a country rich in dinosaur remains!). The supermassive *Futalognkosaurus*—meaning "giant chief of the dinosaurs"—was as heavy as an aircraft carrier.

BRACHIOSAURUS
(BRACK-EE-OH-SORE-US)

Sure, giraffes may have long necks by today's standards, but wait until you meet this guy! Hailing from the late Jurassic period, *Brachiosaurus*—known from the U.S.A. and Tanzania—was about 82 feet (25 m) long and weighed 50 tons (45.4 t). Like other sauropods it sported a superlong neck that it could hold upright to reach nearly five stories high into trees to feed. It got its name, which means "arm lizard," because its front legs were longer than its back legs.

DREADNOUGHTUS
(DRED-NAW-TUS)

This dominant dino's name means "fears nothing"—and for good reason! The 77-million-year-old *Dreadnoughtus schrani* is thought to have weighed as much as 65 tons (59.3 t) and stretched 85 feet (26 m) long, standing two stories tall at its shoulder. Scientists were able to recover an amazing 100 out of about 142 types of bones in *Dreadnoughtus*'s skeleton (excluding the skull), which helped them determine its whopping size.

Meet some record-breaking dinos that were the biggest of their kind.

BIGGEST
ARMORED DINO

ANKYLOSAURUS
(AN-KYE-LOH-SORE-US)

WARNING: Approach with caution. The squat, four-legged *Ankylosaurus* was no fearsome predator, but it was covered in spikes and in defensive armor made from hundreds of bony plates—even on its eyelids! About 20 feet (6 m) long, the largest of the "tanklike" herbivores known as ankylosaurs roamed North American woodlands at the end of the Cretaceous period.

BIGGEST DINO WITH
BIRDLIKE WINGS

ZHENYUANLONG (JEN-HWAHN-LONG)

The 125-million-year-old nearly complete skeleton of this prehistoric raptor was unearthed in northeast China's Liaoning province. Could the largest dino with birdlike wings and feathers ever found actually fly? Scientists think not. It had arms that were short compared with other dinos in its family, and—at about 44 pounds (20 kg)—was pretty heavy. Scientists think the wings might have been for display, like a peacock's.

BIGGEST
PLATED DINO

STEGOSAURUS (STEG-OH-SORE-US)

My, what beautiful ... plates you have! Up to 30 feet (9 m) long and weighing more than 2 tons (1.8 t), late Jurassic *Stegosaurus* was the largest of the plate-backed, plant-eating dinosaurs known as stegosaurs. It sported two rows of staggered, diamond-shaped plates along its neck, back, and tail. Scientists over the years have debated the purpose of the pointy plates but now suspect that they were used for display, perhaps to attract potential mates.

BIGGEST DOME-SKULLED DINO

PACHYCEPHALOSAURUS (PACK-EE-SEF-AH-LOW-SORE-US)

The largest of the pachycephalosaurs ("domed dinosaurs"), late Cretaceous *Pachycephalosaurus* had a supersized skull-cap—about 20 times thicker than other dino skulls. Some experts think these plant-eating boneheads may have used their distinct domes to head-butt each other, but others say the creature's neck was not strong enough to withstand the cranium collisions without breaking. Now that's a head-scratcher!

THE MISSING BONE

Calling all sleuths: It's one of paleontology's biggest mysteries—a dinosaur bone that could hold the clues to the biggest dinosaur that ever lived. But the bone has gone missing!

Way back in 1878, paleontologist Edward Drinker Cope (you can read more about him on page 106–107) claimed to have unearthed a whopping, five-foot (1.5-m)-long vertebra (a part of the backbone) of a dinosaur he called *Amphicoelias fragillimus*. A vertebra that size would have made for one hulking dino— about one and a half times the size of this chapter's winner, "the Titanosaur." But the massive bone is missing from the American Museum of Natural History where the rest of Cope's collection is housed, and no one knows what happened to it.

Some dinosaur experts think that Cope must have made a mistake when he wrote down the size of the bone, claiming it is very unlikely that any dinosaurs got *that* big. Others disagree, saying it's possible that lots of dinosaurs were much bigger than we think they were. Why the uncertainty? It's hard to estimate the size of dinosaurs from parts of skeletons, and many of the fossils we have are of young dinosaurs that might have gotten much bigger if they had lived to be adults.

So, how did a dino bigger than a blue whale—the biggest animal alive today—roam our Earth? That remains a mystery— for now.

MORE MYSTERIES WAITING TO BE SOLVED

HOT OR COLD?

Scientists still aren't sure if dino-saurs were mostly cold-blooded (using outside heat, like from the sun, to stay warm, like modern reptiles) or mostly warm-blooded (keeping their body heat more or less constant no matter the outside temperature, like humans and other mammals). Most scientists these days think that dinosaurs were probably a lot like modern birds and mammals when it comes to body temperature. But some think that dinosaurs could have been something in between cold-blooded and warm-blooded, using several strategies for staying in the comfort zone. For now it's another mystery waiting to be solved.

DAY OR NIGHT?

Were dinosaurs active during the day, getting their beauty sleep at night? Or did they prefer to hunt under the cover of darkness? Many experts think that small mammals were able to survive the Age of Dinosaurs by lying low during the day and coming out only at night, when carnivorous dinos were catching some z's. But some prominent predators, such as *Velociraptor* and *Juravenator,* had eyes that were adapted to let in lots of light, which hints that at least some meat-eating dinos may have slinked through the shadows after all.

VELOCIRAPTOR

HOW MANY DINOSAURS WERE THERE?

Even that's a mystery—and one that may never be solved. Paleontologists find a new dinosaur almost every *week,* and although each new find offers up chances to solve old mysteries, it can also introduce a new puzzle for scientists to solve.

NON-DINO
TITANS

Dinosaurs may have dominated during the Mesozoic, but they weren't the only immense animals of their day. Check out these remarkable, now extinct record breakers that lived during the time of the dinosaurs.

BIGGEST FLYING ANIMAL

WHAT: *Quetzalcoatlus* (KWETS-ul-coe-AT-luss)
WHEN: 70–65 million years ago
WHERE: Plains, woodlands, skies **DIET:** Vertebrates, such as dinosaurs

Quetzalcoatlus was a pterosaur, a group of flying reptiles that people sometimes mistakenly call dinosaurs. This enormous creature was about as tall as a giraffe and had a wingspan of up to 33 feet (10 m)—as wide as an F-16 fighter jet!

BIGGEST BONY FISH

WHAT: *Leedsichthys* (LEEDS-ick-thiss)
WHEN: 176–161 million years ago
WHERE: Oceans **DIET:** Plankton

It may have stretched more than twice as long as a great white shark, but this mega fish was not a fearsome predator. It was a filter feeder, swallowing huge gulps of water and using its bony "gill rakers" to sift out plankton and other tiny animals.

BIGGEST
MARINE REPTILE

WHAT: *Shastasaurus* (shas-tah-SORE-us)

WHEN: 225–208 million years ago

WHERE: Oceans

DIET: Squid, fish

This toothless, short-snouted ichthyosaur (sea-dwelling reptile) grew to more than 66 feet (20 m)—longer than 13 bathtubs end to end!—making it the largest known marine reptile.

BIGGEST SEA TURTLE

WHAT: *Archelon* (ARE-kell-on)

WHEN: 75–65 million years ago **WHERE:** Oceans

DIET: Fish, jellyfish, squid, plants

The immense *Archelon* weighed more than two tons (1.8 t), stretched about 15 feet (4.6 m) from its beak to its tail, and had flippers spanning more than 16 feet (5 m). This sea turtle—whose closest living relative is the leatherback sea turtle (which grows to less than half of *Archelon*'s length)—is thought to have had a life span of 100 years.

MONSTERS
OF THE MESOZOIC

Many dinosaurs were enormous, but one group boasts more bragging rights in this category than all the others. The great sauropods of the Mesozoic era were the biggest land animals ever to have roamed the planet—by a long shot. So how did they get so big? Scientists don't really know for sure, but they have a few ideas. One hypothesis, called the Evolutionary Cascade Model, says that they were able to grow so big because they didn't chew their food. Weird, yes? But the logic makes sense: Because sauropods didn't chew their food, they didn't need big jaws and strong muscles in their heads, so their heads were lighter. Because they didn't have to hold up heavy heads, their necks could grow longer. Longer necks were able to swing around and graze a bigger area without using a lot of energy moving from place to place, so they could eat a lot without spending too much energy. And that's why they were able to get very, very big—or so that argument goes.

LATE CRETACEOUS SAUROPOD ISISAURUS

WHAT'S THE BIG IDEA?

SOME IDEAS about why some dinos got so big are pretty silly. One says that gravity was weaker back then, so it was easier to grow to epic proportions. Or higher oxygen levels in the Mesozoic atmosphere allowed animals to grow bigger. Another holds that there were so many more plants to eat back then that herbivores grew massive at the prehistoric salad bar. Although these hypotheses are fun, and a couple get a few details right, none of these ideas hold up to the cold, hard facts.

CORYTHOSAURUS **SOUNDS** WEREN'T JUST **HOT AIR,** THEY WERE A WAY FOR THESE DINOS TO COMMUNICATE

BONEHEAD

This massive plant-eater may not have been the biggest of the big dinosaurs, but it likely made a very big noise. *Corythosaurus* was a type of hadrosaur (duck-billed dinosaur) that lived about 75 million years ago, in the late Cretaceous period. It was a little over 30 feet (9 m) long and about six feet (almost 2 m) high at the hips, and may have weighed five tons (4.5 t). Its most fantastic feature? It had some really funky headgear. That's how it got its name, which means "helmet lizard."

If you think *Corythosaurus* looks goofy on the outside, you should see it on the inside. In 2008, scientists used a CT scanner—the same machine that doctors use to get an inside look at human patients—to study the insides of those curvy bones. They found that because of the shape of *Corythosaurus's* inner ear, the dino would have been able to hear very low-frequency sounds. And the hollow bones would have helped them make deep and loud noises. A chatty herd of corythosaurs may have sounded something like the cello section warming up before a symphony.

Why did they make all that racket? Possibly to attract mates. But corythosaurs could also have bellowed out warnings of approaching predators to other corythosaurs— which would have been a big deal because these dinos had no natural defenses.

CORYTHOSAURUS LIVED IN BIG HERDS LIKE MODERN WILDEBEEST OR BUFFALO.

BATTLE OF THE BRAWN

Who will prevail in our fantastical matchups?

WINNER

Experts put these sauropods at roughly the same size—about five times the length of a twin-size bed—but its soaring neck spikes make early Cretaceous *Amargasaurus* a more imposing sight than late Triassic *Riojasaurus*.

RIOJASAURUS vs. **AMARGASAURUS**

Triceratops is the clear winner here, its 30 feet (9.1 m) easily surpassing *Pentaceratops*'s 22 feet (6.7 m) or so. But hey, let's give *Pentaceratops* props for having more horns: five to *Triceratops*'s three.

WINNER

PENTACERATOPS vs. **TRICERATOPS**

WINNER

UTAHRAPTOR **vs.** DEINONYCHUS

At about 20 feet (6 m) long, *Utahraptor* was around twice as big as *Deinonychus*. But don't feel bad for the "little" loser. *Deinonychus* had plenty of other things going for him; like *Utahraptor*, he also had a set of sharp claws suitable for snaring and slicing prey.

Maiasaura, aka the "good mother lizard," may have been too big to sit on her eggs; she had to cover them with leaves instead! But her 30-foot (9-m) frame was no match for the 40-foot (12-m)-long hadrosaur *Charonosaurus!*

WINNER

CHARONOSAURUS **vs.** MAIASAURA

TSINTAOSAURUS **vs.** PACHYCEPHALOSAURUS

This is a heady matchup! At about 15 feet (4.6 m) long, dome-headed *Pachycephalosaurus* was no small fry. But, at twice that length, unicorn-horned *Tsintaosaurus* pulls out ahead.

WINNER

BY THE NUMBERS

LOST AND FOUND

Remains of dinosaurs and other prehistoric creatures have been discovered on every continent on Earth. And more and more are found all the time! Here's what just a few spots around the world have yielded in spectacular ancient finds.

Gobi desert, Mongolia
More than 80 genera of dinosaurs

Liaoning Province, China
Approximately 60 species of plants, 90 species of vertebrates, and 300 species of invertebrates identified

Ischigualasto and Talampaya Natural Parks, Argentina
Around 56 known genera (plus many more species of vertebrates) and 100+ species of plants

Dinosaur Provincial Park, Alberta, Canada
More than 44 species, 34 genera, and 10 families of dinosaurs

DOMAIN

KINGDOM

PHYLUM

CLASS

ORDER

FAMILY

GENUS

SPECIES

FOSSILS ARE THE TRACES OR **REMAINS OF ORGANISMS** THAT WERE **ONCE LIVING.**

Organize those **DINOS!**

If you collect stamps or baseball cards or even have a lot of books or video games, you know how important it is to have a system for organizing things. The same is true for animals! There are billions of living things (organisms) on Earth, and taxonomy is the system scientists use to classify them into groups—kind of like a huge imaginary filing cabinet. There are eight levels of classification. The top, or broadest group, is called a domain. The bottom, or most specific group, is called a species. In the drawer just above species is genus—two or more are called genera.

TIP: Here's a sentence to help you remember the order of the classifications: **D**ear **K**ing **P**h**i**llip **C**ame **O**ver **F**or **G**ood **S**oup.

COLOSSAL CROCS

t's been a while, crocodile! Relatives of modern "crocodilians" (crocodiles, alligators, caimans, and gharials) first appeared more than 200 million years ago, in the late Triassic period. By the middle of the Cretaceous period (about 100 million years later) some had—like their dinosaur cousins—evolved into supersized predators.

Today's largest crocodilian, the saltwater crocodile, generally reaches an incredible 17 feet (5.2 m) and 1,000 pounds (454 kg), but try this on for size: 112 million years ago, a now extinct croc-like reptile twice as long and about 20 times as heavy was prowling the prehistoric rivers of the Sahara. *Sarcosuchus imperator* (or "flesh crocodile emperor") lay in wait for its unsuspecting prey, lunging out and chomping down with its massive five-foot (1.5-m)-long jaws.

It might not be surprising to hear that prehistoric crocs of this stunning size were able to take down some pretty hefty prey; bite marks found on the bones of some tyrannosaurs have matched the teeth of the 70-million-year-old *Deinosuchus* ("terror crocodile"), a 10-ton (9-t) predator thought to have been as long as *T. rex*. Larger prey was ripped into pieces, and smaller prey was (gulp!) swallowed whole.

CROCODILIANS AND THEIR **EXTINCT RELATIVES** (TOGETHER CALLED CROCODYLOMORPHS) ARE PART OF THE SAME GROUP (ARCHOSAURS) THAT ALSO INCLUDES **DINOSAURS** AND **BIRDS.**

CROCODILIANS

GROUP: **REPTILES**

CURRENT RANGE: **ASIA, AFRICA, AUSTRALIA, THE AMERICAS**

HABITAT: **TROPICAL HABITATS; NEAR RIVERS, LAKES, WETLANDS, AND SOME SALTWATER AREAS**

NUMBER OF LIVING SPECIES: **23**

PENTACERATOPS (PEN-TA-SER-AH-TOPS)

DROMICEIOMIMUS (DRO-MISS-EE-OH-MEE-MUS)

BIG-AT-A-GLANCE

1 **BIGGEST HEAD**

This big-headed herbivore is thought to have had the largest skull of any land animal, with one "heady" skull fossil reaching more than 10 feet (3 m) long! *Pentaceratops*—which means "five-horned face"—roamed wooded plains in North America during the late Cretaceous period.

2 **BIGGEST FOOTPRINTS**

Remember the gigantic sauropods? They also had big feet! Scientists believe a sauropod dino weighing more than 44 tons (40 t) and stretching 82 feet (25 m) long made the huge footprints discovered in a tiny French town in 2009. The tracks spanned up to 4.9 feet (1.5 m)—so wide you could likely lay down inside them!

3 **BIGGEST DINO EYES**

Dromiceiomimus had eyes that were about three inches (7.6 cm) wide—about the diameter of a baseball! This two-legged omnivorous ornithomimid (ostrich-like dinosaur) ate vegetation as well as meat when it roamed Canada 74 to 70 million years ago, possibly using its enormous eyes to hunt at night or in low light.

SAUROPOD FOOTPRINTS

AN OUT-OF-THIS-WORLD FIND

In 2012, a group of Cretaceous-period dinosaur footprints pressed into mud were found on the grounds of NASA's Goddard Space Flight Center in Greenbelt, Maryland, U.S.A. Scientists believe the dinosaurs that made the prints were adult and juvenile nodosaurs—a group of heavily armored, spiked plant-eaters—and an ornithopod, from a group of medium to large herbivorous dinos.

4 BIGGEST LAND PREDATOR IN EUROPE

Jurassic period *Torvosaurus gurneyi* stretched 33 feet (10 m) and topped the scales at four to five tons (3.6–4.5 t)! Fragmentary remains from Germany and the United Kingdom hint at the presence of other (perhaps larger) predatory dinosaurs in Europe.

5 LONGEST NAME

Say it five times fast: *Micropachycephalosaurus!* This compact creature from the late Cretaceous may have the longest name of any dinosaur, but at just two feet (0.6 m) long and less than 10 pounds (4.5 kg)—about the size of an average house cat—it is actually one of the smallest that ever existed.

6 LONGEST TAIL

Dinosaurs are divided into two basic groups: the lizard-hipped (saurischian) dinos and the bird-hipped (ornithischian) dinos. The 10-foot (3-m), two-legged herbivore *Leaellynasaura* may have had the longest tail of any of the ornithischians—about three times as long as its head, neck, and body combined! *Leaellynasaura* lived 106 million years ago in what is now southern Australia.

TORVOSAURUS
(TORE-VO-SORE-US)

LEAELLYNASAURA
(LEE-EL-IN-A-SORE-A)

LONG LIVE THE DINOS?

DURING A **GROWTH SPURT,** APATOSAURUS MAY HAVE GAINED CLOSE TO **SIX TONS** (5.4 T) **A YEAR!**

APATOSAURUS

ACCORDING TO ONE STUDY, THE GROWTH RATE OF T. REX WAS ABOUT THE SAME AS MODERN BIRDS.

Sure, many dinos got plenty big, but does that mean they had big life spans, too? Scientists once thought that dinosaurs might have lived for a hundred years or more. How'd they figure that? They compared dinosaur growth rates to the growth rates of modern-day reptiles, like tortoises, which are very slow-growing animals and can live 150 years or more. But recently, scientists made a groundbreaking discovery: They found growth rings in dinosaur bones. We know from studying the bones of modern vertebrates (animals with backbones) that growth rings are made when new bone is added to the outside of the bones as an animal grows, sort of like growth rings in a tree. Now scientists can take thin slices of dinosaur bone and study the rings to figure out how old the dinosaur was when it died. That doesn't tell us how long a dinosaur *could* have lived, but it does offer important clues about the growth rate of the animal, so scientists can make more accurate estimates.

So did dinosaurs really live for more than a hundred years? Probably not. Based on the growth rings, experts estimate that the large herbivores, like *Brachiosaurus,* probably lived at most about 70 to 80 years, and the (relatively) smaller meat-eaters, like *T. rex,* probably lived for around 30 years or so. They may not have set any longevity records, but they sure could fill their birthday cakes with candles.

TITANIC TRACKS!

Check out these footprints from prehistoric and modern times. Can you match the big-footed behemoth to the track it left behind?

A

BEAR

2

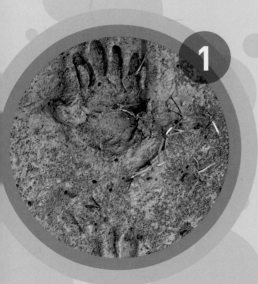

1

B

SAUROPOD

ANSWERS
A:3; B:2; C:1; D:5; E:4

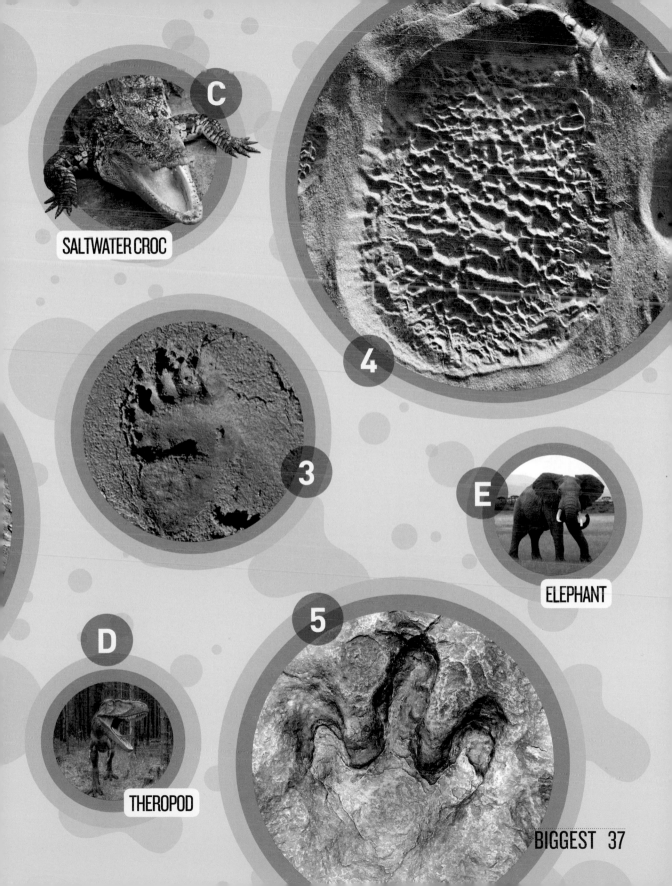

C

SALTWATER CROC

4

3

E

ELEPHANT

D

5

THEROPOD

IT'S NO MINOR MATTER— SOME OF THE COOLEST DINOSAURS WERE ALSO SOME OF THE SMALLEST.

You didn't think a dinosaur had to be big to be in this book, did you? Tiny dinos can still be fast, ferocious, and fascinating from top to tail. Turn the page to meet the small wonders.

SCUTELLOSAURUS

RESEARCHERS HAVE DETERMINED THAT
MICRORAPTORS'S FEATHERS WERE **IRIDESCENT,**
WHICH MEANS THEY HAD A METALLIC SHEEN LIKE THE
FEATHERS OF **PEACOCKS** AND **HUMMINGBIRDS.**

MICRORAPTOR

(MY-CROW-RAP-TORE)

TYPE: DROMAEOSAUR

DIET: CARNIVOROUS

LIVED: 128 TO 124 MYA

RANGE: CHINA

WEIGHT: ABOUT 2 POUNDS (0.9 KG)

LENGTH: 3 FEET (0.9 M)

HEIGHT: 1 FOOT (0.3 M)

The smallest known dinosaur, this compact carnivore was remarkable for having fully formed feathers on both its front and rear limbs—the kinds of "flight" feathers we see on today's birds. But scientists do not believe *Microraptor* took flight by flapping its wings. About the size of a crow, this tree-dwelling dino is thought to have used its sharp, curved claws to climb up trees and its primitive wings to glide from branch to branch in pursuit of its favorite prey: insects, lizards, and small mammals.

Researchers used wind-tunnel experiments to determine that the diminutive dino would have been able to leap from a height of 65 to 100 feet (19.8–30.5 m)—about the size of trees in the part of China where it lived during the early Cretaceous period. Glide on, little buddy!

Look out below! You would have towered over these tiny dinos.

PARVICURSOR
(PAR-VI-KURSE-OR)

Some scientists believe the pigeon-size *Parvicursor* could have been the smallest dinosaur, but this late Cretaceous carnivore from Mongolia (whose name means "small runner") is known from only a partial skeleton. So for now, it'll have to settle for second place. *Microraptor*—for which there are an estimated 300 fossil specimens for scientists to learn from—takes our tiniest crown.

COMPSOGNATHUS
(KOMP-SOG-NAH-THUS)

This petite prehistoric predator was only about the size of a turkey, but it was definitely no chicken! *Compsognathus* was a fierce, fast-running, late Jurassic hunter with sharp teeth, clawed hands, and a tail more than half the length of its body, which helped it stay balanced as it chased and overtook small prey like lizards.

LESOTHOSAURUS
(LE-SOH-TOH-SORE-US)

You can't catch me! *Lesothosaurus* evolved around 200 million years ago in what is now southern Africa. Based on its bone structure, scientists believe the 3.3-foot (1-m) herbivore was a speedy little creature: It had elongated feet and shins that were longer than its thighs—leg proportions similar to those of fast-running animals today, such as ostriches.

MINMI
(MIN-MEE)

Nope, that's not "mini me"! *Minmi*—whose name comes from the area in Australia where it was discovered—was a slow-moving early Cretaceous herbivore whose body (including its belly!) was covered with small, hard, rounded armor plates. *Minmi* was only about 2.5 feet (0.8 m) tall and likely ate fruit, seeds, and other plant parts.

These dinos win big for being some of the smallest of their kind!

SMALLEST SAUROPOD

EUROPASAURUS (YOO-ROPE-AH-SORE-US)

You know that sauropods like our "biggest" winner, the Titanosaur, were the largest land-dwelling animals ever on Earth, so it's hard to imagine that any of them could have been as compact as the 154-million-year-old *Europasaurus!* Scientists believe that this particular species—which fossils show reached "only" up to 20 feet (6.2 m)—stayed relatively small due to limited food resources on the islands where it lived (in present-day Germany).

SMALLEST TYRANNOSAUR

DILONG (DYE-LONG)

Would you believe that this tiny tyrannosaur is related to the towering *T. rex*? It is! Dating from about 128 million years ago, the feathered *Dilong* was one of the earliest known tyrannosaurs and also one of the smallest: It was only about one-eighth as long as the colossal king of the dinos.

SMALLEST
ARMORED DINO

SCUTELLOSAURUS
(SKOO-TELL-OH-SORE-US)

Scutellosaurus is an early relative of the tanklike *Ankylosaurus*. Only four feet (1.2 m) long and weighing twice as much as a house cat, the 196-million-year-old herbivore sported more than 300 protective plates—each smaller than a bottle cap—on its skin from neck to tail, which would have provided it with some much-needed protection from predators.

SMALLEST **CERATOPSIAN**

AQUILOPS (ACK-WILL-OPS)

The oldest known relative of *Triceratops* found in North America is also one of the smallest ceratopsians (horned and frilled dinos) ever! This early Cretaceous critter weighed about as much as the average rabbit—or only .02 percent the heft of *Triceratops*.

PINT-SIZE
PALEONTOLOGISTS

DAISY MORRIS SURROUNDED BY
HER COLLECTION OF FOSSILS,
SHELLS, AND BONES

Dinos come in all shapes and sizes, from wider than a whale to no bigger than a bird. But did you know that the people who discover prehistoric creatures can be pretty small, too? Daisy Morris was only four years old in 2008 when she found a bone while walking along the beach near her home on the Isle of Wight in England. The bone was from a species of pterosaur that had not yet been discovered. The best part? Scientists named the new species—a dinosaur cousin that lived during the Cretaceous period—after Daisy: *Vectidraco daisymorrisae*. How cool is that?!

You may be amazed to learn that lots of kids have found fossils! Wylie Brys was about the same age as Daisy when, in 2014, he made his find in Texas, U.S.A. He was kicking around a construction site with his father and dug up a bone from a nodosaur, an armored herbivore from the late Jurassic. Another young dino hunter, Diego Suarez, was seven in 2004 when he went to southern Chile on a research expedition with his geologist parents. There he found the bones of a plant-eating relative of *T. rex*, which was also named in his honor: *Chilesaurus diegosuarezi*. So what makes kids so good at finding fossils? Who knows? Maybe being closer to the ground helps. Whatever the reason, keep your eyes peeled the next time you're out exploring; you never know when you might uncover your own prehistoric treasure!

MORE ON THEIR FANTASTIC FINDS!

NODOSAURUS

Wylie kicked up a 100-million-year-old nodosaur fossil, which would be exciting in any case, but especially so because he found it in Texas, where not many land-dwelling dinosaurs have been found. *Nodosaurus* was a 13- to 20-foot (4- to 6-m)-long armored herbivore that lived from the late Jurassic to the early Cretaceous.

VECTIDRACO DAISYMORRISAE

Daisy's find was a very big deal: It wasn't a dinosaur, but a pterosaur—a toothless flying reptile that lived in the Cretaceous period, soaring over the heads of dinosaurs. Daisy's find was a totally new species of this frequent flier.

CHILESAURUS DIEGOSUAREZI

Diego's famous find has been described as a jigsaw dinosaur. Why? A vegetarian cousin of *T. rex*, the 10-foot (3-m)-long theropod had its more famous relative's tiny arms, but with blunt fingers instead of claws. Its back feet looked more like *Diplodocus* than *T. rex*, and its pelvis somewhat resembles that of a *Triceratops*.

LITTLE LIMB LINE-UP

Try not to laugh: Some of the largest, most daunting dinosaurs had bizarrely tiny arms.

THE LONG— AND SHORT— OF IT

Take a good look at this line-up. Notice anything funny about their form? Yup: Their arms are minuscule compared with the size of their bodies. Why did these immense late Cretaceous predators grow so big everywhere but their front limbs, you ask? Their arms were way too short to reach their mouths or to provide much protection if they fell forward while running, and some scientists believe it's unlikely they could have used them to grab prey. So what could their abbreviated arms possibly have been useful for? Scientists have a few ideas: to rip apart carcasses, perhaps, or as meat hooks while feeding, or even as a way to get up after lying or sitting down. Researchers also believe that the small front limbs may have been "vestigial": body parts that were once useful but were used less and less— and therefore became smaller and less useful— as the species evolved. Have you ever heard that humans have vestigial body parts? We do! The wisdom teeth, tailbone, and appendix are all considered vestigial.

TYRANNOSAURUS REX
(TYE-RAN-OH-SORE-US RECKS)

Towering *T. rex* has a fearsome reputation, with many people assuming that the well-known hunter-scavenger was the biggest dino ever. It wasn't, but still: It was indeed one of the biggest meat-eating dinos that ever lived. *T. rex's* grabbers may have been on the small side—about the same length as an adult human arm—but they sported sharp claws and were strong and well built.

MAJUNGASAURUS
(MAH-JOONG-AH-SORE-US)

Despite its short, stubby forelimbs, 23-foot (7-m)-long *Majungasaurus* was once the dominant predator on what is now the island of Madagascar. Indeed, this bold, broad-skulled flesh-eater even preyed on members of its own species!

CARNOTAURUS (CAR-NO-TORE-US)

You might expect that a 2.2-ton (2-t) dino whose name means "flesh-eating bull"—and who had two intimidating horns sticking out above each eye—would also boast some pretty impressive front limbs to whack you with: no dice. The quick-running carnivore had teeny, four-fingered hands and arms shorter than a human's!

BRAIN TEASER

What's the scoop on smarts?

STEGOSAURUS

DESPITE being small, the crow is no birdbrain. On some tasks, it does as well as the notoriously brainy great apes.

HORSES do a lot for humans—lug stuff around, take us places, jump over things when we ask them to. But they're not all brawn! They have also shown the ability to learn and think: Scientists recently taught horses to communicate by training them to point at symbols with their muzzles.

Being called a "pea brain" might not be an insult after all—it just depends on how big you are! It turns out having a small brain doesn't always mean an animal isn't smart. And having a big brain doesn't mean it is. More important than the size of the brain is how big the brain is compared to the size of the animal's body. The bigger an animal's body, the more brain it needs to operate that body. So if you're a big animal with a small brain—like *Stegosaurus*—you won't have enough noodle power to do much more than the basics (eat, reproduce, and defend yourself from predators). On the other hand, a crow is a small animal, but it is pretty clever—sharper on average than the much larger horse.

When scientists try to estimate how smart a dinosaur was, they also use something called EQ. That stands for "encephalization quotient" and is a way of comparing the sizes of dinosaur brains to brains of modern animals of similar sizes to determine their smarts.

SOME SCIENTISTS THINK THAT GETTING ALONG WITH OTHERS TAKES MORE BRAINPOWER THAN LIVING ALONE, SO DINOSAURS THAT LIVED IN SOCIAL GROUPS WERE PROBABLY MORE INTELLIGENT THAN LONERS.

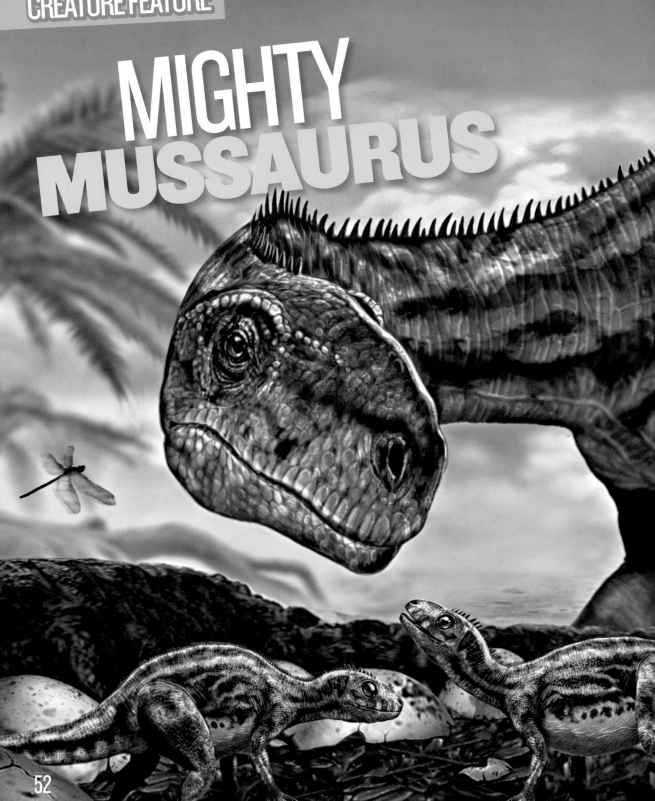

MIGHTY
MUSSAURUS

MUSSAURUS WAS ONE OF THE EARLIEST DINOSAURS. IT LIVED ABOUT 215 MILLION YEARS AGO, IN THE LATE TRIASSIC.

The smallest dinosaur skeleton ever found was discovered in the 1970s in Argentina in a nest of eggs and hatchlings. It was only eight inches (20.3 cm) long. Because of its scant size, scientists named the species *Mussaurus,* which means "mouse lizard." But the bones were deceiving: More than 30 years later, when adults of the same species were found, their size surprised scientists. They learned that as adults, those mouse-size *Mussaurus* babies could grow to as much as 10 feet (3 m) long. Still not that huge for a dinosaur, but way bigger than a mouse!

The *Mussaurus* skeletons proved remarkable in other ways, too. When the skeletons of the babies were first found, paleontologists didn't know a lot about the nesting behavior of dinosaurs—very few babies and nests had been found. The find showed scientists that, just like people, baby dinosaurs didn't look very much like grown-ups. *Mussaurus* also helped scientists learn more about the family lives of dinosaurs. For example, dino parents at least sometimes stuck around to take care of their babies before they left the nest. Who said giant prehistoric reptiles couldn't be sweet?

SMALL BUT SPEEDY

They may be small, but they had to be fast—outrunning a predator may have been the only way for these tiny dinos to survive! But which would beat the other in a race?

LESOTHOSAURUS VS. LINHENYKUS

WINNER

Lesothosaurus takes the medal in this contest because it was not only fast, it also had long legs that would have easily outpaced the smaller *Linhenykus*. Tough luck this time, *Linhenykus*.

MINMI VS. SCUTELLOSAURUS

WINNER

Two armored dinos going head to head in a foot-race might not sound like the most exciting event to watch—but *Scutellosaurus*'s speed would surprise you. The dino was lightly built and walked on two legs, allowing it to easily outpace the much slower herbivore, *Minmi*.

WINNER

ARCHAEORNITHOMIMUS **VS.** **MICRORAPTOR**

Microraptor was small, but speed wasn't its thing. Instead of soaring like an eagle, it glided like a kite—pretty, but not fast. The speedy *Archaeornithomimus* would take this race without breaking a sweat.

COMPSOGNATHUS **VS.** **SCANSORIOPTERYX**

WINNER

Compsognathus was speedy enough to catch the lizards it liked to eat, and *Scansoriopteryx* was better suited to the more leisurely habit of climbing trees, making this competition a no-contest win for *Compsognathus*.

DINOS
TOP TO BOTTOM

Check out how many of these dinos end-to-end it would take to reach the remarkable length of the Titanosaur.

MICRORAPTOR:
41

LESOTHOSAURUS:
37

MINMI :
12

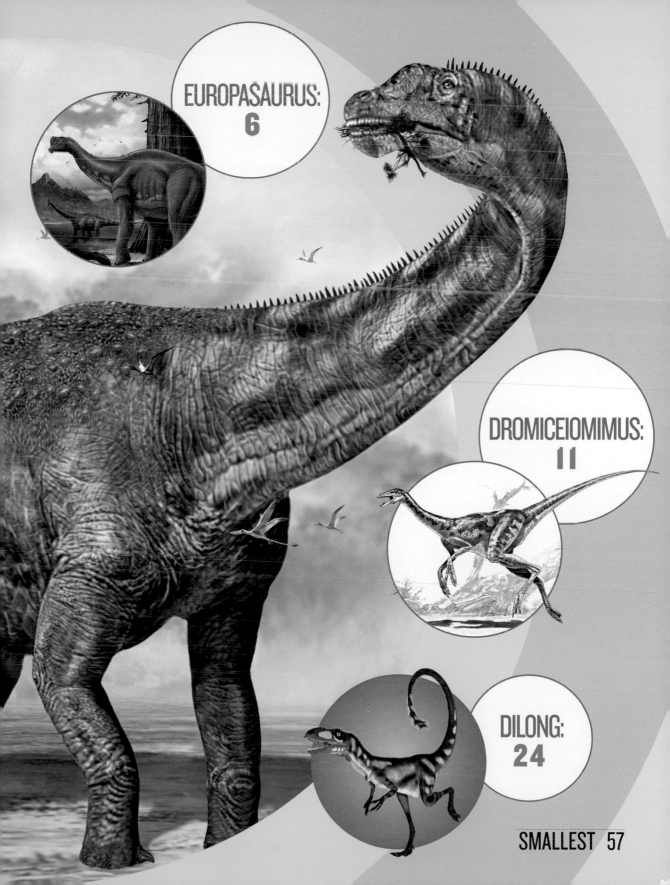

EUROPASAURUS:
6

DROMICEIOMIMUS:
11

DILONG:
24

TINY BUT MIGHTY

Here's the buzz: Bees—which scientists believe have been around for about 120 million years—play an important role in agriculture and horticulture around the world. These small, flying insects that invade picnics and sometimes sting us (ouch!) are actually critical to our survival. How can that *bee*? As the winged wonders buzz around, they transfer seeds and pollen from one flower to another, helping plants grow and make food. About one out of every three foods we eat depends directly or indirectly on honeybee pollination, including more than 130 fruits and vegetables—some of which may regularly make it onto your dinner plate. Bees help produce familiar fare such as oranges, carrots, blueberries, and broccoli, and they also pollinate food that is eaten by the animals people eat. If these hard-working bees were to stop spreading seeds, many plants (including food crops) would die—so be glad they stuck around!

Bees may have survived the mass extinction that killed the dinosaurs, but they are facing a serious threat today: Sadly, bees are vanishing at an alarming rate in a phenomenon called Colony Collapse Disorder, in which they leave their hives and never return. Why is this happening? Scientists believe it is due to a combination of reasons, including the use of pesticides, the presence of parasites, the loss of their habitats to development, and global climate change. Measures are now being taken by governments and by farmers to investigate and to try to prevent the decline in honeybee populations. We need these little creatures for our survival—and that's no small matter.

BEES

GROUP: **INVERTEBRATES**

CURRENT RANGE: **WORLDWIDE, EXCEPT ANTARCTICA**

HABITAT: **GARDENS, FARMS; AREAS WITH PLANTS, FLOWERS, AND CROPS**

NUMBER OF LIVING SPECIES: **MORE THAN 20,000**

POLLEN IS MOVED FROM PLANT TO PLANT BY **BEES** AND OTHER POLLINATORS— INCLUDING **BATS, BIRDS, BUTTERFLIES,** AND OTHER INSECTS—AS WELL AS BY **WIND.**

SMALL-AT-A-GLANCE

DROMICEIOMIMUS
(DRO-MISS-EE-OH-MEE-MUS)

TETHYSHADROS
(TEH-THISS-HAY-DROSS)

① SMALL SPEEDSTER

Beep, beep! Paleontologists believe that a group of long-legged dinos called the ornithomimids (meaning "bird mimics") were the fastest dinosaurs that ever lived. It is thought that one of these, *Dromiceiomimus*, may have been able to run up to 50 miles an hour (80 km/h)—slightly faster than the fastest living animal on two legs: the ostrich.

② SMALLEST NORTH AMERICAN PREDATOR

The smallest meat-eating dinosaur yet known from North America, the chicken-size, razor-clawed *Hesperonychus* used its rows of daggerlike teeth to chomp on the insects and small mammals it found in the forests and swamps of the late Cretaceous period.

③ SMALLEST DUCK-BILLED DINOSAUR

Back in the late Cretaceous, *Tethyshadros* inhabited an island in an area that is now Italy. This island dweller's restricted range is believed to have contributed to its small size compared with its bigger "mainland" relatives.

HESPERONYCHUS (HES-PUH-RUH-NIE-KUS)

FRUITADENS
(FROO-TAH-DENZ)

BEE HUMMINGBIRD

4 SMALLEST BRAIN

Stegosaurus's brain may have been the smallest relative to body size of any dinosaur. Although it probably wasn't ideal for quantum physics, this tiny thinker did help the plate-backed plant-eater survive in the late Jurassic; the part used for smell was relatively large, an asset that helped *Stegosaurus* sniff out its dinner.

5 SMALLEST BIRD-HIPPED DINO

Squirrel-size *Fruitadens* nabs the title of the smallest of the ornithischian (or "bird-hipped") dinosaurs, a group that includes dinos like *Stegosaurus* and *Triceratops*. Although it sounds like this diminutive dino was named after its favorite food, the late Jurassic omnivore was actually named after the area where it was found.

6 SMALLEST MODERN-DAY DINO

Modern-day birds actually evolved from dinosaurs—which makes birds, well, dinosaurs! That would make the smallest present-day dino the bee hummingbird, the smallest bird in the world.

STEGOSAURUS (STEG-OH-SORE-US)

BRAIN IN THE BUTT?
MYTH BUSTED!

Some researchers once thought that *Stegosaurus* had a "second brain" in its rump. Scientists knew it had a puny brain for such a large beast, so they wondered if maybe another thinker in its hind end coordinated its back legs and tail or maybe sped signals from the rear part of the body to the main brain. Paleontologists have since learned this wasn't true; dinos had only one brain.

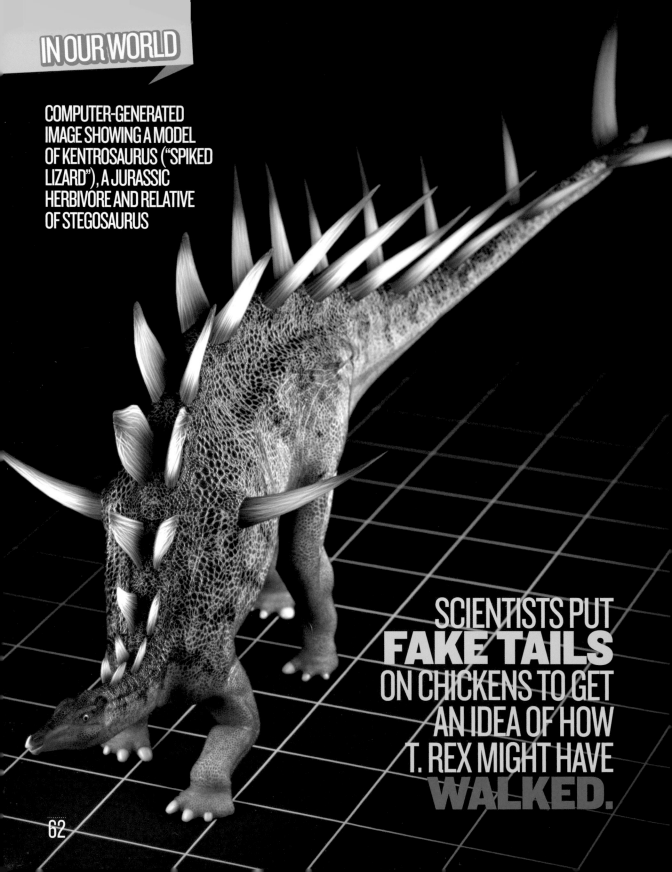

COMPUTER-GENERATED IMAGE SHOWING A MODEL OF KENTROSAURUS ("SPIKED LIZARD"), A JURASSIC HERBIVORE AND RELATIVE OF STEGOSAURUS

SCIENTISTS PUT **FAKE TAILS** ON CHICKENS TO GET AN IDEA OF HOW T. REX MIGHT HAVE **WALKED.**

CUTTING SCIENCE DOWN TO SIZE

Fossilized bones can help paint a picture of what an animal looked like, but determining how an ancient creature moved is a much trickier task. Did they run, hop, or just shuffle along? It's difficult to tell by looking at their bones alone, so scientists turned to a high-tech solution to tackle this dino-size conundrum. First, they use laser scanners to make a 3-D model of the dinosaur skeleton on a computer. Then—using marks left on the bones as a guide—they add in the muscles. Finally, they test various types of gaits (running, hopping, trotting) to see which ones might work and which ones would put too much stress on the animal's bones. The result is a computer simulation that brings long-extinct dinosaurs to life—often with surprising results.

Before computer modeling, scientists thought that the giant *Argentinosaurus* might have had trouble walking because it was so big. But when they crunched the data using a computer program, it turned out that the big guy was able to stroll along at about five miles an hour (8 km/h)—about the pace you might manage on a brisk walk around the block. Not record setting, but plenty fast enough for a giant that's too big for most predators to eat.

PALEONTOLOGISTS ASSEMBLE FRAGMENTS OF THE FOSSILIZED BONES OF A TITANOSAUR.

PAST AND PRESENT

MATCH THE DIMINUTIVE DINOSAUR TO THE MODERN ANIMAL IT'S CLOSEST TO IN SIZE.

TURKEY

B

4

SCUTELLOSAURUS

1

FRUITADENS

F

RABBIT

A

C

DOG

SQUIRREL

E

CROW

2

COMPSOGNATHUS

3

MINMI

6

AQUILOPS

D

TIGER

5

MICRORAPTOR

SMALLEST 65

WARNING: **DEADLY** DINOS WITH **TERRIBLE TEETH** AND **COLOSSAL CLAWS** AHEAD. PROCEED WITH **CAUTION!**

What makes a dino deadly? Is it massive size? Wielding weapons like knife-sharp teeth and claws handy for tearing into meaty prey? Or maybe it's speed that wins the day? Read on to discover the different ways dinos can be deadly.

YANGCHUANOSAURUS

SPINOSAURUS

(SPINE-OH-SORE-US)

This meat-eater was the longest predatory dinosaur ever to have roamed the Earth. Known for the spectacular spines that formed a sail along its back, *Spinosaurus* was almost as long as a bowling lane from nose to tail—making it even longer than the fearsome *T. rex*—and was equipped with strong arms and three huge claws on each hand.

But *Spinosaurus* reigns supreme for another reason: This Cretaceous carnivore could catch prey in the water—its preferred hunting ground—as well as on land. With paddle-like feet and with nostrils that sat far back on its long, crocodile-like snout (allowing it to breathe even when its head was partly underwater), it likely spent a lot of time in rivers and lakes, using its colossal jaws and sharp teeth to snatch lungfish, sawfish, sharks, and other huge fish, including a car-size coelacanth, *Mawsonia*.

TYPE: **SPINOSAURID**

DIET: **CARNIVOROUS**

LIVED: **112 TO 97 MYA**

RANGE: **NORTH AFRICA**

WEIGHT: **8.8 TONS (8 T)**

LENGTH: **55 TO 56 FEET (16.8–17.1 M)**

THE RUNNERS-UP ...

Beware! These deadly dinos slashed, crushed, and tore their prey to pieces.

DEADLIEST BITE FORCE

TYRANNOSAURUS REX (TYE-RAN-OH-SORE-US RECKS)

T. rex had the strongest bite of any land animal that has ever lived: It could bear down on its prey with a maximum force of nearly 12,800 pounds (5,806 kg)—a crushing weight about the same as that of an adult *T. rex*'s body! Scientists once found part of a *T. rex* tooth embedded in the spine of a hadrosaur (a large plant-eating dino). *Ouch!*

DEADLIEST **TEETH**

ALLOSAURUS (AL-OH-SORE-US)

This 28-foot (8.5-m) carnivorous killing machine roamed North America 150 million years ago. *Allosaurus* sported a huge, deep skull with long, sawlike teeth sharp enough to pierce skin and muscle, allowing it to tear large chunks of flesh out of some of its favorite prey: plant-eating dinos. Paleontologists have even discovered what they believe to be an *Allosaurus* bite mark on a *Stegosaurus*'s neck plate!

DEADLIEST **RAPTOR**

UTAHRAPTOR (YOO-TAH-RAP-TORE)

This fast-moving fright was about three times the length of a bed and taller than the average adult man. The biggest of all the dromaeosaurs—or "raptors"—the ultra-deadly *Utahraptor* hunted herbivores 125 million years ago using its speed, strong jaws, sharp teeth, and nine-inch (23-cm)-long curved claws to overtake and shred its powerless prey.

DEADLIEST **FRONT FANGS**

MASIAKASAURUS(MAH-SHEE-AH-KAH-SORE-US)

Allosaurus may be the winner for all-around chilling chompers, but *Masiakasaurus* sported some deadly daggers. This dog-size carnivore had front teeth that stuck straight out of its mouth, which scientists believe it may have used to spear lizards and fish some 70 million years ago.

MORE RUNNERS-UP ...

Feast your eyes on these determined and deadly dinos.

DEADLIEST GIANT SPRINTER

GIGANOTOSAURUS (JIG-AH-NO-TOE-SORE-US)

Talk about life in the fast lane! Some experts estimate that this 40-foot (12.2-m)-long Cretaceous carnivore could clock 30 miles an hour (48 km/h) when chasing down its prey. That would be faster than the estimated speed of a similarly huge and fearsome predator: *T. rex*. It's difficult for scientists to calculate speed for these giants, however, because we don't have two-legged animals this big running around today—lucky for us!

DEADLIEST **TOES**

DEINONYCHUS (DIE-NON-NY-KUSS)

Talk about slicing and dicing! The raptor *Deinonychus* (whose name means "terrible claw") was equipped with five-inch (12.7-cm)-long talons on its second toes. Scientists believe that the agile, fast-moving Cretaceous carnivore probably used these cutting claws to slash, gut, and kick its prey powerless and may have also used them to pin its prey to the ground —like modern-day raptors. How did it keep its built-in blades so sharp? It could flip them up while walking to keep them from dragging on the ground.

DEADLIEST **PLANT SHREDDER**

GRYPOSAURUS (GRIP-OH-SORE-US)

If plants could run, they would have surely sprinted away from this super shredder! Herbivorous late Cretaceous *Gryposaurus* came at them with a huge appetite for vegetation; it had a three-foot (0.9-m)-long head with 300 teeth (and plenty more replacements at the ready in its jawbone), which it used to devour bushes and small trees.

DEADLIEST **SNIFFER**

SAURORNITHOLESTES (SORE-OR-NITH-OH-LESS-TEASE)

At less than three feet (0.9 m) tall and six feet (1.8 m) long, this dino may have been on the small side compared to other predators of the late Cretaceous, but it was equipped with a honkin' advantage: a highly developed sniffer. Besides being quick and agile, *Saurornitholestes sullivani* had a super sharp sense of smell that enabled it to effectively sniff out potential prey.

DEADLIER BY THE DOZEN

With their sickle-shaped retractable claws, surprising speed and agility, and relatively large brains compared to their bodies, prehistoric raptors like *Deinonychus* and *Utahraptor* were superefficient killing machines. But bringing down the sometimes massive (and often spiked and armored) herbivores they hunted would have been a big—and dangerous—job, even for these toothy terrors.

Some paleontologists think that raptors were successful predators because they hunted in packs—like wolves or lions do today. *Deinonychus* teeth have been found among the skeletons of several tenontosaurs (an herbivore twice the size of *Deinonychus*), and at on e site at least three *Deinonychus* were found alongside a *Tenontosaurus*. *Deinonychus*-like tracks found in China show the animals walking together in the same direction and even swerving to avoid bumping into each other, making it look as if these dinosaurs weren't competing but instead were living and hunting together.

Although the evidence for pack hunting had been mounting, it hadn't been strong until 2015, when a block of sandstone found in Utah gave scientists the break they'd been looking for. It contained at least six *Utahraptor* skeletons along with fragments of an iguanodontid, an herbivore. Paleontologists believe the plant-eater got stuck in some quicksand and several *Utahraptors* went in after it. Or perhaps the raptors chased the iguanodontid into the bog and they all got stuck. Either way, this remarkable find has strengthened the case that some of the most vicious dinosaurs could become even more deadly by working in packs.

ATTENTION ALL HERBIVORES

These dinosaurs are highly suspected of pack-hunting behavior.

DEINONYCHUS
LAST SEEN: **110 MYA**

UTAHRAPTOR
LAST SEEN: **125 MYA**

VELOCIRAPTOR
LAST SEEN: **70 MYA**

YANGCHUANOSAURUS
LAST SEEN: **160 MYA**

DINO DEFENSES

Scientists don't know for sure whether plant-eating dinos used their amazing attributes to battle their carnivorous cousins, but these herbivores were armed with some pretty wicked ways they could have used to defend themselves.

ARMOR: GASTONIA

(GAS-TONE-EE-AH)

Prickly *Gastonia* was covered in heavy, defensive armor. To protect it from the strong jaws of meat-eaters it had four horns on its head, thick layers of bone shielding its brain, rows of spikes sticking out from its back, and a tail with triangular blades running along each side.

SPIKES: KENTROSAURUS

(KEN-TROH-SORE-US)

Stand back! This cousin of *Stegosaurus* had paired spikes along its tail, which it could swing at attackers with great speed. One paleontologist estimated that *Kentrosaurus* could have swung its treacherous tail fast enough to shatter bones!

CLUB TAIL:
ANKYLOSAURUS

(AN-KYE-LOH-SORE-US)

Steer clear! *Ankylosaurus* possessed a heavy, knobby tail that it could have used to whack attackers. It may not have totally protected the tanklike late Cretaceous dino from a determined *T. rex*, but a serious swing could have generated enough force to do some real damage to its rival reptile.

WHIP TAIL:
DIPLODOCUS

(DIH-PLOD-UH-KUS)

Some scientists think this late Jurassic giant's tail—about half the length of its 90-foot (27-m) body—could have been used like a whip and swished at high speeds, creating a loud noise that would send potential predators running.

HORNS: TRICERATOPS

(TRI-SER-UH-TOPS)

There's no evidence *Triceratops* ever used its horns to combat late Cretaceous snack-craving carnivores. But scientists do believe the famous three-horned creature used its frills and horns in battle with other members of its species.

ONE-TWO

What *really* killed off the dinosaurs? For a long time, most experts agreed that an asteroid the size of a small city that slammed into Earth 65 million years ago was solely responsible for their demise. The impact set off a series of events that wiped out a majority of the planet's land and sea creatures. But when it came to doing in the dinos, that asteroid may have had some help. Scientists have found evidence that volcanic eruptions—in what is now west-central India, in an area called the Deccan Traps—had been going on for 250,000 years before the asteroid hit, and the eruptions increased dramatically in the 50,000 years before the dinos bit the dust. All that lava spewing out would have put plenty of dangerous chemicals in the air, contributing to global warming, making the oceans more acidic, and killing off many of the animals that the big predators ate. So the asteroid strike may have been just the last straw for the dinosaurs. Hundreds of thousands of years of intense volcanic activity had already done a lot of damage to their ecosystem, setting them up for the next big blow. Scientists call it a one-two punch: Take that ... and this!

PUNCH

FAR OUT!

Over the years there have been some **totally weird hypotheses** about what caused the dinosaurs' ultimate demise:

DINOSAURS WENT **BLIND** FROM SPENDING TOO MUCH TIME **LOOKING AT THE SUN** AND STUMBLED OVER CLIFFS TO THEIR DEATHS.

CATERPILLARS ATE UP ALL THE PLANTS, LEAVING DINOSAURS **NOTHING TO EAT.**

DINOSAURS GOT **TOO MANY CAVITIES** AND **COULDN'T CHEW** THEIR FOOD.

THEIR **BRAINS** KEPT **GETTING SMALLER** UNTIL THEY WERE **TOO DUMB** TO SURVIVE.

FEROCIOUS
IN THE FAR EAST

Plant-eaters in Asia during the late Jurassic must have cowered in terror from *Yangchuanosaurus*, a deadly dino stretching almost as long as a bus. With its big and bony head, the knob on its snout, and its long, knifelike teeth, it must have been one scary-looking dino. Using a thick tail almost half the length of its body for balance, *Yangchuanosaurus* had two very muscular legs, big claws on each of its three toes, and short arms that boasted still more killer claws. Although it terrorized local herbivores, such as the nearly doubly long *Mamenchisaurus*, *Yangchuanosaurus* could also use its massive claws and powerful jaws to rip apart any dead animals it happened across. *Yangchuanosaurus* got its dinner—dead or alive.

THE FIRST YANGCHUANOSAURUS **FOSSIL** WAS FOUND BY A **CONSTRUCTION WORKER** WHILE EXCAVATING FOR A DAM.

YANGCHUANOSAURUS PROBABLY WEIGHED **4,000 POUNDS** (1,814 KG).

DEADLY VS. DEADLIER

Which of these dinos was more menacing in the Mesozoic?

T. rex was a bone-crunching beast to behold, but sail-backed *Spinosaurus* delivered its viciousness at greater speed and in a larger package. Plus, it could take down prey on land and in the water (see pages 68–69), making us declare *Spinosaurus* the winner by a narrow margin (though some experts we talked to disagreed).

WINNER

T. REX **VS.** SPINOSAURUS

ANKYLOSAURUS **VS.** CONCHORAPTOR

Though *Conchoraptor* was a meat-eater with a powerful beak, *Ankylosaurus* is our winner: The plant-eater was bigger and had the advantage of a bone-crushing club tail capable of taking out carnivores trying to turn him into a tasty snack.

WINNER

DRAW

GIGANOTOSAURUS **vs.** **CARCHARODONTOSAURUS**

Carcharodontosaurus's jagged teeth could strike fear into many a rival, but its close relative *Giganotosaurus* had equally nasty chompers. Because the two mega-predators were roughly the same size—and likely equally menacing to their prey—this contest is a draw!

DEINONYCHUS **vs.** **CARNOTAURUS**

WINNER

Deinonychus and *Carnotaurus* were both skilled predators with excellent vision—a major advantage when stalking prey. But at 25 feet (7.6 m) long, *Carnotaurus* would have loomed over the 10-foot (3-m)-long *Deinonychus*, winning *Carnotaurus* the trophy in this deadly duel.

KILLING MACHINES AND THEIR SPECTACULAR SPECS

Sprint speed of *Giganotosaurus*: **30 miles** an hour (48 km/h)

=

About the speed of a **white-tailed deer**

BITE FORCE OF *T. REX'S* JAWS: **12,800 POUNDS** (5,806 KG) =

THREE TIMES THAT OF A **GREAT WHITE SHARK** (4,000 POUNDS (1,814 KG))

Height of *Spinosaurus's* **record-breaking spines:** 7 feet (2.1 m)

=

Taller than an average **adult male**

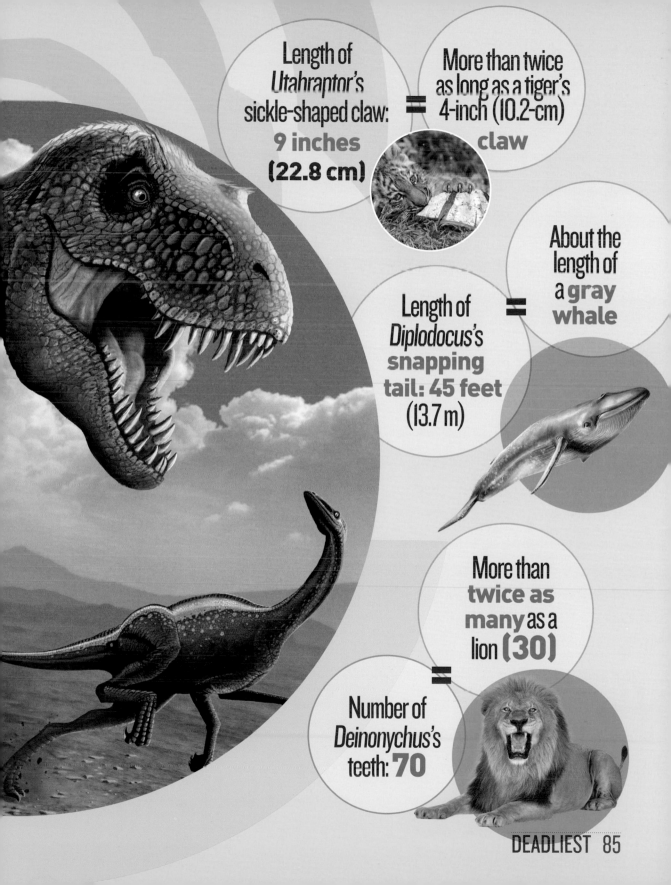

Length of *Utahraptor's* sickle-shaped claw: **9 inches (22.8 cm)**

=

More than twice as long as a tiger's 4-inch (10.2-cm) claw

Length of *Diplodocus's* **snapping tail: 45 feet (13.7 m)**

=

About the length of a **gray whale**

More than **twice as many** as a lion (**30**)

=

Number of *Deinonychus's* teeth: **70**

SUPERLATIVE SHARKS

Perfection takes time. And sharks have had plenty of time to evolve into the supereffective predators they are today. Fossil records show that these fierce fish emerged between 455 and 420 million years ago, meaning they were hunting in Earth's ocean for a couple of hundred million years before the earliest known dinosaurs! Not only do the ancestors of modern sharks pre-date the dinosaurs, they also pre-date mammals, amphibians, and even insects. The long-living ocean dwellers even survived multiple mass extinctions, including the event 251 million years ago that wiped out as many as 95 percent of Earth's species. Today's big sharks (including bull sharks, hammerheads, and everyone's favorite fearsome fish, the great white) are known as apex predators, meaning that they're at the top of the ocean's food chain—a position that helps them keep ecosystems in balance. And although on rare occasions sharks have attacked humans with whom they have crossed paths, people are not their preferred prey: They'd rather dine on fish and marine mammals, thank you very much.

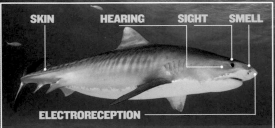

SKIN   HEARING   SIGHT   SMELL

ELECTRORECEPTION

WHAT MAKES SHARKS SUCH EFFICIENT PREDATORS?

Electroreception: A shark's sensitive snout can detect the electrical fields of other animals underwater—even tiny ones.

Smell: Some sharks can sniff out prey at one part per 10 billion—the equivalent of one drop in an Olympic-size swimming pool.

Sight: Sharks have really good eyesight—even in the dark—because their pupils dilate and contract to change the amount of light they let in.

Hearing: Sharks have supersensitive hearing, able to detect prey moving about two football-field lengths away.

Skin: Tiny "teeth" called dermal denticles cover sharks' skin and reduce drag while the shark is swimming.

GROUP: **FISH**

CURRENT RANGE: **FROM COASTAL WATERS TO THE OPEN OCEAN**

HABITAT: **OCEANS WORLDWIDE**

NUMBER OF LIVING SPECIES: **MORE THAN 400**

SCIENTISTS DISCOVERED SHARKS LIVING INSIDE AN UNDERWATER VOLCANO.

DEADLY-AT-A-GLANCE

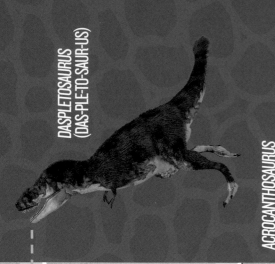

DASPLETOSAURUS
(DAS-PLE-TO-SAUR-US)

ACROCANTHOSAURUS
(AK-RO-KANTH-UH-SAWR-US)

1 DEADLIEST EARLY TYRANNOSAUR

Ten million years before *T. rex*, *Daspletosaurus* was the top predator in the floodplains of North America. Bite marks in the found skulls of these 30-foot (9-m)-long, 3.3-ton (3-t) colossal carnivores suggest the powerful-jawed "frightful lizards" may have tangled with each other over territory, food, or the title of dominant dino.

2 DEADLIEST DINO DOWN UNDER

Dating back 110 million years, "Lightning Claw" is the largest carnivorous dinosaur ever found in Australia. Its nickname (it doesn't yet have an official name) comes from Lightning Ridge, New South Wales, Australia, where its bones were found, and from its large, sharp claws, which would have been used like grappling hooks to seize prey.

3 DEADLIEST SAUROPOD CHASER

Fossilized footprints found by scientists indicate that the 40-foot (12.5-m)-long early Cretaceous predator *Acrocanthosaurus* (or a closely related form) hunted and chased down larger plant-eating dinosaurs—such as the massive plant-eating sauropods—by running alongside and lunging at its prey. It is estimated that *Acrocanthosaurus* may have been able to run up to 25 miles an hour (40 km/h)!

LIGHTNING CLAW

PHENOMENAL FIND

In 2015, an Australian cattle farmer spraying weeds stumbled across a fantastic fossil: the most complete lower jawbone ever found of a *Kronosaurus queenslandicus*, which lived in Australian waters about 110 million years ago. The magnificent mandible (jaw) was just over five feet (1.6 m) long and belonged to a still-growing *Kronosaurus*; fully grown, the creatures' jaws reached about 8.5 feet (2.6 m).

**KRONOSAURUS
(CROW-NO-SORE-US)**

4

DEADLIEST SNOUT

Majungasaurus was equipped with a broad, short snout that allowed it to subdue its prey—such as sauropods—by biting and holding on. Scientists have discovered *Majungasaurus* bones featuring bite marks from other *Majungasaurus*—which they believe is evidence that the late Cretaceous carnivores were cannibals (meaning they preyed on their own species!).

**MAJUNGASAURUS
(MAH-JOONG-AH-SORE-US)**

5

DEADLIEST SEA PREDATOR

Named after the Greek mythological figure Kronos, who (gulp!) ate his own children, *Kronosaurus* was a 33-foot (10-m)-long Cretaceous plesiosaur (marine reptile). It likely swam with its mouth open, gobbling up fish, mollusks, and other unfortunate creatures that crossed its path.

6

DEADLIEST PHOLIDOSAUR

Supersized *Sarcosuchus* is sometimes called a croc, but it was actually a prehistoric crocodile-like reptile called a pholidosaur. Thought to have been about as long as a bus and twice as heavy as a minivan, long-extinct *Sarcosuchus* prowled rivers looking for fish and other prey to crush in its formidable jaws.

**SARCOSUCHUS
(SAR-KOH-SOO-KISS)**

VEG

MOST **DINOSAURS** WERE **HERBIVORES.**

HEAD

S ome of the deadliest dinos are members of a group called the coelurosaurs—fast and fierce predators that survived by stalking and attacking plant-eaters that roamed the Mesozoic world. Sure, like many modern meat-eaters, such as lions and hyenas, the opportunistic predators sometimes scavenged for meat, eating already dead animals. But whether their prey was dead or alive, coelurosaurs were strictly meat-eaters. Or were they?

By studying the fossilized poop, stomach contents, and teeth of coelurosaurs, scientists discovered that many of these predators may have enjoyed a tasty salad once in a while, too. What's even weirder: Some of these dinosaurs that we usually think of as fierce predators had kicked their meat habit altogether and gone totally vegetarian! Over time, their teeth became flatter and more wedge-shaped, much more useful for tearing into a tasty bush than into a meaty dinosaur. Some species even lost most of their teeth and developed birdlike beaks instead, and some had stones in their stomachs to help grind up the plants they ate. It's still a mystery why some groups of meat-eating dinosaurs would have evolved to be mostly veggiesaurs, but one idea is that they adapted to take advantage of the abundance of flowering plants that emerged during the Cretaceous period. We may never know why they kicked their meat habit while relatives like *T. rex* and *Velociraptor* were full-time carnivores. Talk about going green!

DEADLY DINO
TRIVIA

How much have you learned about this chapter's deadly dinos? Decide whether these declarations are true or false.

1

T. REX had the strongest bite strength of any land animal that has ever lived.

2

DEINONYCHUS kept its five-inch (12.7-cm)-long talons sharp by scratching them on prehistoric pine trees.

4

ACROCANTHOSAURUS was a solitary hunter that moved slowly to creep up on prey.

3

DIPLODOCUS may have used the cracking sound made by its whiplike tail to scare off attackers.

5

GIGANOTOSAURUS was the biggest dinosaur ever.

6

SPINOSAURUS was longer than *T. rex.*

UTAHRAPTOR'S front teeth pointed outward to spear prey.

8

7

TRICERATOPS used its frills and horns to fight with other *Triceratops.*

9

ALLOSAURUS bite marks have been found on a ptero-dactyl's neck bone.

10

SAURORNITHOLESTES'S secret hunting weapon was its powerful sniffer.

CHAPTER 4

ALL DINOSAURS
BIG, SMALL, ARMORED, PLATED, FEATHERED, FEROCIOUS, OR OTHERWISE ARE **A LITTLE WEIRD** IN THEIR OWN WAY.

But the dinos in this chapter will definitely make you stare a little bit harder and scratch your heads a little bit longer. Will you agree with these peculiar picks? Turn the page to discover the weirdest dinos!

QIANZHOUSAURUS

WEIRDEST 95

The winner for weirdest dino is so zany, even its discovery was puzzling! In 1965 in the Gobi desert, fossil hunters found a pair of eight-foot (2.4-m)-long arms sporting three eight-inch (20-cm)-long claws. To what mysterious creature were they once attached? Scientists could only imagine. Nearly five decades later, they had located enough other fossils of *Deinocheirus mirificus* ("unusual terrible hand") to finally develop a clearer picture of the uncanny animal.

Deinocheirus walked tall on two legs and was as gigantic as *T. rex* ... and yet, some-how, looks like it would have been a lot less intimidating to creatures in the late Cretaceous. Maybe it's the peculiar proportions—the long, pointed head; the ducklike, toothless snout; the huge, gangly arms (the longest known of any animal on two legs!); the sail-like hump on its back; the big belly—or maybe it's the mash-up of all of the above. That's one quirky creature!

DEINOCHEIRUS
(DYE-NUH-KYE-RUS)

TYPE: **ORNITHOMIMOSAUR**

DIET: **OMNIVOROUS**

LIVED: **70 MYA**

RANGE: **MONGOLIA**

WEIGHT: **13,000 POUNDS (6,000 KG)**

LENGTH: **36 FEET (11 M)**

HEIGHT: **16 FEET (4.9 M)**

Meet some dinos that defy imagination.

THE MYSTERY
DIGIT

IGUANODON
(IG-WAN-OH-DON)

Cool thumb, bro'. Scientists are not entirely sure why *Iguanodon* had spiked thumbs, but some hypotheses are that this enormous early Cretaceous plant-eater used them for close-range defense against predators, in combat with other *Iguanodon*, or for (yawn) digging into fruits and seeds. That's one strange spike!

THE COLOSSAL **CLAW**

THERIZINOSAURUS (THERE-IH-ZIN-OH-SORE-US)

Therizinosaurus's approximately three-foot (0.9-m)-long talons—the longest claws known of any animal—look like they could have made mincemeat of potential prey. But *Therizinosaurus* was actually an herbivore that researchers believe used its claws to pull down tree branches for snacking. The massive, five-ton (4.5-t) dino likely still used its monster claws to defend itself against predators in late Cretaceous Mongolia, where it lived 70 million years ago.

THE DRACULA **DINO**

PEGOMASTAX (PEG-OH-MAST-AX)

A beak like a parrot, teeth like a vampire, and quills like a porcupine? Yup, it's really weird. This tiny, two-legged, 200-million-year-old herbivore was less than two feet (0.6 m) long and weighed about as much as a kitty cat. *Pegomastax*'s fierce-looking fangs might lead you to believe they did some damage in the Jurassic, but this pint-size plant-eater likely stuck to nuts and seeds.

THE ORIGINAL **BIG BIRD**

GIGANTORAPTOR (GEE-GANT-OH-RAP-TER)

Feathered, toothless, and towering, *Gigantoraptor* is the biggest oviraptorosaur ever found: 3,000 pounds (1,400 kg) and (at its shoulder) twice the height of a man. Despite its odd and outsized appearance, the omnivorous *Gigantoraptor* was probably not a fearsome predator; the 26-foot (8-m)-long chickenlike creature likely ate plants—though it possibly also swallowed some smaller animals whole.

MORE RUNNERS-UP ...

These curious creatures will make you do a double take.

THE CURIOUS CROWN

REGALICERATOPS PETERHEWSI (REE-GAH-LIH-SEH-RAH-TOPS)

Regaliceratops belongs to a group of horned dinosaurs called chasmosaurines—whose members usually have small nose horns but large eye horns and simple, shieldlike frills. You'd never guess it, though: With its tiny eye horns, large nose horn, and an elaborate crown of bony spikes around the back of its skull, *Regaliceratops* is much more like a different group of horned dinosaurs called the centrosaurines. Pretty weird, given that *Regaliceratops* lived two million years after the centrosaurines died out!

THE PINOCCHIO DINO

QIANZHOUSAURUS (SHEE-AHN-ZHOO-SORE-US)

We cannot tell a lie! Owing to its thin, long nose, *Qianzhousaurus* has indeed been nicknamed "Pinocchio rex." The 66-million-year-old carnivore was smaller than its cousin *T. rex*, whose snout was shorter and more muscular. *Qianzhousaurus*'s elongated jaw was weaker than that of the "tyrant lizard king," meaning it probably favored smaller prey.

THE UNLIKELY VEGETARIAN
CHILESAURUS (CHEE-LAY-SORE-US)

Theropods were usually meat-eating dinos (such as tyran-nosaurs) that chased after their prey and tore it to pieces. But unlike its large-headed, thick-necked, sharp-toothed, meat-eating cousins, theropod *Chilesaurus diegosuarezi* had a small head, a thin neck, a horny beak, and flat teeth just right for chewing plants. This cool contrar-ian was named after Diego Suarez, the seven-year-old boy who found its bones in Chile while out hiking with his parents (see pages 46–47).

THE FREAKY CHICKEN
ANZU WYLIEI (AHN-ZOO)

Sporting feathers on its upper arms; a tall, bony crest; and a sharp-edged, birdlike beak, *Anzu* also had a long lizardlike tail and a jaw that could slide back and forth to cut up vegetation or small animals. Scientists have nicknamed it "the Chicken from Hell" because of where its bones were found: the Upper Cretaceous Hell Creek Formation in North and South Dakota, U.S.A.

WEIRDEST 101

WALL WALKERS

Dinosaurs may seem like the superheroes of the Mesozoic—but could they walk on walls? You might think so if you went to Bolivia and looked at one of the largest sets of dinosaur tracks ever discovered. In 1994, paleontologists found more than 5,000 footprints from at least six different types of dinosaurs. The weird thing about this site is that the tracks are on the side of a limestone cliff that rises almost straight up out of the ground like a giant rock wall—as if the dinosaurs were wall walkers!

Turns out it's all a trick of Mother Earth—dinos definitely could not walk up walls. How'd it happen? Well, what is now a vertical wall of rock was the bottom of a shallow lake when these tracks were made in the late Cretaceous. These types of movements happen when tectonic plates in Earth's crust move around on top of softer rock underneath. When the plates crash into each other, the edges of the plates bend and fold, creating mountains and, in this case, a near vertical wall out of what was once a lake bed—giving us an extremely cool display of dinosaur tracks.

CONTINENTAL COLLISION

What is now the Andes mountain range—one of the longest mountain ranges on Earth, with peaks up to 22,000 feet (6,705 m)—used to be flat, warm, and wet land. The same plate shifting that created the dinosaur wall created this massive mountain range.

It has been a long time since the Andes formed, but the plates underneath the continent are still moving. Even now, the area has lots of volcanoes and earthquakes that are caused when the big continental plates crash into one another, creating gaps for hot volcanic gases to erupt and fault lines that cause earthquakes. Even though the Age of Dinosaurs is long over, the movements of the planet that changed the world are still occurring.

DINO TRACKS IN THE ANDES, IN CHILE

TRACKS AT CAL ORCKO, NEAR SUCRE, BOLIVIA

REAL-LIFE SEA MONSTERS

While dinos were the dominant reptiles on land, other remarkably weird reptiles were ruling the seas.

NAME: *Albertonectes* (al-BER-to-NEK-teez)
LIVED: 83-71 million years ago
LENGTH: 36 feet (11 m) **ATE:** Fish, squid

Talk about sticking your neck out! The school-bus-size plesiosaur *Albertonectes* had a neck longer than the rest of its body, with more neck bones (76!) than any animal we know of. It moved through oceans by flapping its four flippers and using its small jaws to munch on squid, fish, and other prey.

NAME: *Liopleurodon*
(LIE-oh-PLOOR-oh-don)
LIVED: 165–150 million years ago
LENGTH: 23 feet (7 m), but it may have grown much larger
ATE: Fish, large squid, marine reptiles

Although their relatives the plesiosaurs (like *Albertonectes*) had long necks and small heads, the pliosaurs had short necks and huge heads. The faster-moving pliosaurs, with their big, strong jaws and huge, spiked teeth, were better equipped to ambush larger prey.

NAME: *Ophthalmosaurus*
(off-THAL-mo-SORE-uss)
LIVED: 165–150 million years ago
LENGTH: 16 feet (4.9 m)
ATE: Mollusks, squid, fish

Ophthalmosaurus had the widest eyes relative to body length of any animal that ever lived; each was about the diameter of a soccer ball! The sleek, one-ton (950-kg) ichthyosaur is thought to have been able to see well and hunt in deep, dark water, using its long, thin jaw to snatch fish, squid, and other marine animals.

NAME: *Mosasaurus* (MOSE-ah-SORE-us)
LIVED: 70–65 million years ago
LENGTH: 49 feet (15 m)
ATE: Fish, shellfish, squid

Mosasaurus was a gigantic, ferocious predator and a close relative of modern-day snakes and lizards. The croc-like carnivore used its long, strong, flat tail and its four flippers to navigate through late Cretaceous oceans. Scientists believe that *Mosasaurus* wasn't much of a long-distance swimmer but that it was able to speed through the water in short bursts to ambush prey.

THE BONE WARS

Two of the most successful fossil hunters ever were Edward Drinker Cope and Othniel Charles Marsh, whose "competitive spirit" could be characterized as ... a little weird. What began as a friendly rivalry between these two 19th-century paleontologists turned into a nasty feud as each tried to one-up the other.

Both men played dirty: Marsh hired spies to keep track of what Cope was doing, and Cope publicly accused Marsh of misusing government funds. One time, Marsh paid workers at Cope's digs to send their finds to him rather than to Cope. On another occasion Cope described in a scientific journal a giant plesiosaur that he named *Elasmosaurus*. But in his rush to publish he made a big mistake. He put the skull on the wrong end of the skeleton! Marsh made a huge deal of his rival's butt-headed blunder, totally humiliating Cope and intensifying their dislike of each other.

The feud, which has become known as the "bone wars," damaged both men personally and professionally. Because Cope and Marsh were more interested in outdoing each other than in doing good science, they both made a lot of mistakes. Much of the work they did had to be redone by later paleontologists. But at least one good thing came of their obsession: a huge amount of fossil finds.

REAL OR FAKE?

Ever heard of a big-bodied dino called *Brontosaurus*? Well, guess what? For more than a century it was thought to be a big a mistake! For a long time, the American Museum of Natural History in New York had a display of an *Apatosaurus* skeleton with a *Camarasaurus* head on it. When a properly constructed *Apatosaurus* came along, Marsh, always in a hurry to get the jump on his rival Cope, thought it was a brand-new dino and named it *Brontosaurus*—making the misnamed skeleton one of the most famous dinosaurs that never existed! Or did it? In another twist to this already wacky story, scientists now think Marsh may have been right all along. A recent study found more than seven differences between *Apatosaurus* and *Brontosaurus*—maybe enough to qualify *Brontosaurus* as a species all its own, and redeem Marsh's reputation.

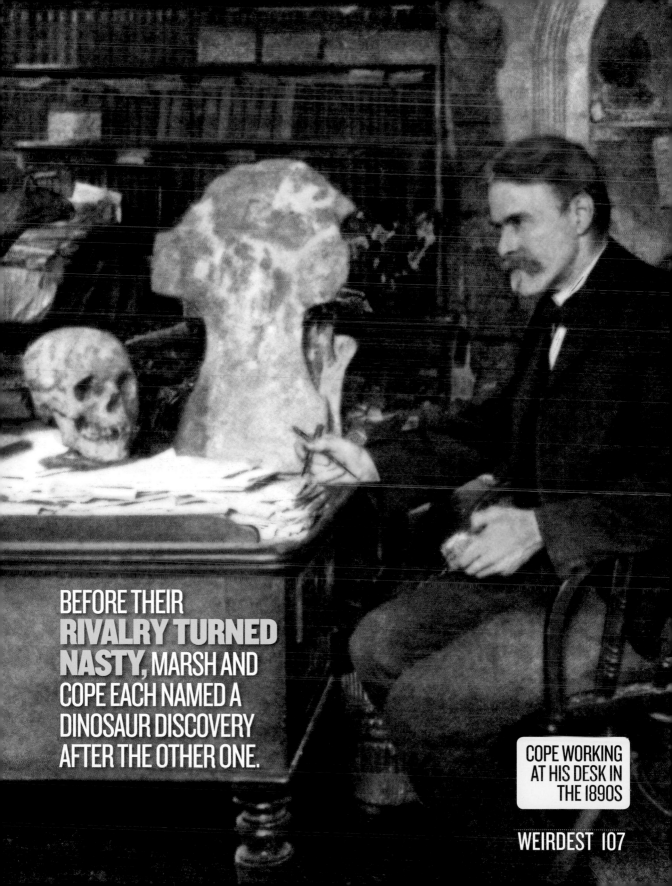

BEFORE THEIR **RIVALRY TURNED NASTY,** MARSH AND COPE EACH NAMED A DINOSAUR DISCOVERY AFTER THE OTHER ONE.

COPE WORKING AT HIS DESK IN THE 1890S

RUSSELL'S DINOSAUROID HAS **NO TEETH**, BUT IT DOES HAVE A NAVEL.

108

TROODON

DINOSAUROID: SUSPICIOUSLY HUMAN

Birds evolved from a group of dinosaurs called theropods. The "avian dinosaurs" survived to modern times, but the rest—the "non-avian dinosaurs"—did not. But what if they had? Scientists sometimes wonder about this kind of thing—even dreaming up ideas of what the prehistoric creatures might have looked like today. One such scientist, Dale Russell, when he was curator of vertebrate fossils at Canada's National Museum of Natural Sciences, went so far as to build a life-size model of what late Cretaceous predator *Troodon* might have been like if it had survived extinction and continued to evolve.

Russell's imaginary creature, which he calls dinosauroid, walked upright, had large forward-facing eyes (like humans), and three humanlike fingers on each hand. Dinosauroid also had a language, which sounded something like birdsong. Like many imagined drawings of hypothetical extraterrestrials, Russell's creation was heavily influenced by the human form. Could humanlike dinos really have evolved? Most scientists think not. Instead, intelligent dinosaurs likely would have evolved into shapes that were more like, well, dinosaurs, with a horizontal posture and a long tail—or even become something totally different that we can't even imagine. Of course, no one really knows what *Troodon* would look like if it had continued to evolve—but it sure is fun to let the imagination run wild!

IN ONE BOOK WRITTEN A FEW YEARS AFTER RUSSELL UNVEILED HIS MODEL, THE WRITER THOUGHT THAT **DINOSAUROID WAS ACTUALLY A RECONSTRUCTION OF A REAL DINOSAUR.**

BATTLE OF THE
BIZARRE

The competition is stiff when it comes to weirdness among dinos. Do you agree with the winners listed below?

WINNER

WEIRDEST FACE

With eyes that big, *Ophthalmosaurus* looks like it just glimpsed a ghost! But you can't ignore the peculiar mouth of *Nigersaurus*, whose flat muzzle—filled with more than 500 teeth—was more suited to mowing the lawn than mugging for glamour shots. Say CHEESE!

NIGERSAURUS VS. OPHTHALMOSAURUS

GIGANTORAPTOR VS. TYLOSAURUS

WINNER

WEIRDEST HABIT

Gigantoraptor descended from carnivores but is believed to have been an herbivore. *Tylosaurus* swallowed sharks whole. Scarfing down giant fish is definitely out of the ordinary, but you've got to admit that a raptor that doesn't eat meat is beyond bizarre—a clear win for *Gigantoraptor*.

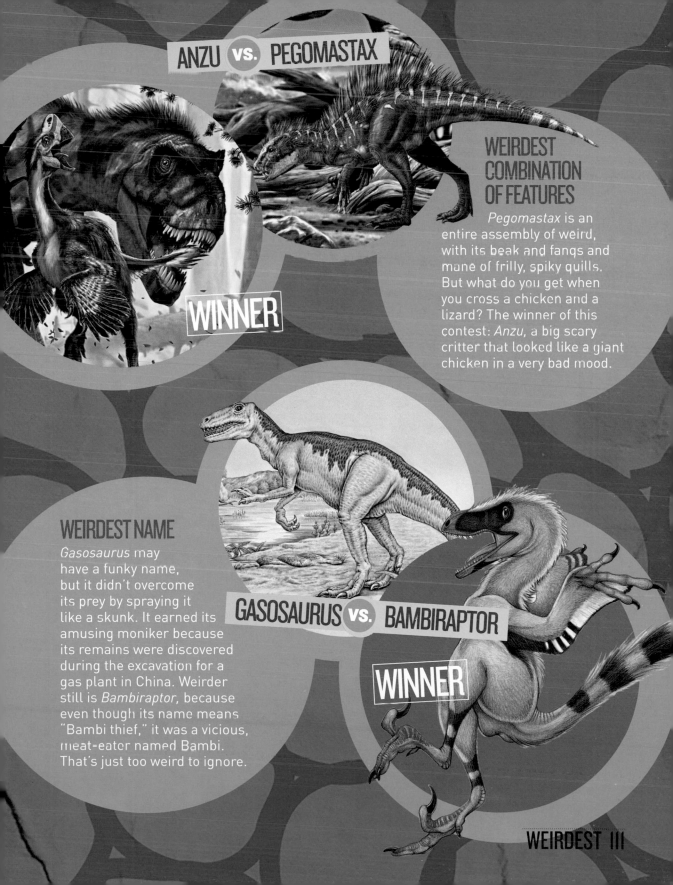

ANZU vs. PEGOMASTAX

WINNER

WEIRDEST COMBINATION OF FEATURES

Pegomastax is an entire assembly of weird, with its beak and fangs and mane of frilly, spiky quills. But what do you get when you cross a chicken and a lizard? The winner of this contest: *Anzu*, a big scary critter that looked like a giant chicken in a very bad mood.

WEIRDEST NAME

Gasosaurus may have a funky name, but it didn't overcome its prey by spraying it like a skunk. It earned its amusing moniker because its remains were discovered during the excavation for a gas plant in China. Weirder still is *Bambiraptor*, because even though its name means "Bambi thief," it was a vicious, meat-eater named Bambi. That's just too weird to ignore.

GASOSAURUS vs. BAMBIRAPTOR

WINNER

HOW LONG AGO WAS THAT?

One of the weirdest things about dinosaurs is how long ago they lived. So long that it's really hard to imagine. Take a look at when these familiar animals appeared on Earth—and how much time passed between some key appearances.

MAMMOTHS

TYRANNOSAURUS REX

65 MILLION YEARS AGO
(LATE CRETACEOUS)

5 MILLION YEARS AGO

125 MILLION YEARS AGO
(EARLY CRETACEOUS)

200,000 YEARS AGO

IGUANODON

HOMO SAPIENS

EORAPTOR

228 MILLION
YEARS AGO
(LATE TRIASSIC)

210 MILLION
YEARS AGO
(LATE TRIASSIC)

MEGALOSAURUS

166 MILLION
YEARS AGO
(MIDDLE JURASSIC)

STEGOSAURUS

159 MILLION
YEARS AGO
(LATE JURASSIC)

COELOPHYSIS

PLATYPUS SPUR

THE PUZZLING
PLATYPUS

When British scientists first laid eyes on a platypus in the late 18th century, some thought the bizarre-looking creature had to be a hoax. You can't really blame them: The platypus is one of nature's most delightfully odd animals—a hodgepodge in both appearance and behavior. Descended from an ancestor that split from all other mammals around 150 million years ago, the native Australian animal has a bill and webbed feet like a duck; a wide, flat tail like a beaver; and a thick, furry body like an otter. It forages in shallow water for insects, crustaceans, and worms, which it stores in "cheek pouches" until rising to the surface to eat them. And whereas mammals almost always give birth to live young, the platypus is one of only two kinds of mammals that lay eggs instead. (Echidnas are the other.)

As if all this weren't weird enough, males of the species are actually venomous! The peculiar platypus can use the sharp pointed spurs on its back feet to inflict a toxic blow to defend itself against approaching enemies or to assert itself against fellow males when competing for mates. Although being spurred by a platypus would be super painful, its venom is not considered life-threatening to a healthy human.

SPECIES NAME:
ORNITHORHYNCHUS ANATINUS

GROUP: **MAMMALS**

CURRENT RANGE: **EASTERN AUSTRALIA, DOWN TO TASMANIA**

HABITAT: **NEAR RIVERS, STREAMS, AND LAKES**

A PLATYPUS STORES **BODY FAT** IN ITS TAIL IN CASE **FOOD** BECOMES **SCARCE.**

AUSTRALIANS ARE SUCH FANS OF THE **PLATYPUS** THEY EVEN PUT THE **UNCONVENTIONAL MAMMAL** ON THEIR **20-CENT COIN.**

XENOCERATOPS
(ZEE-NO-SEH-RAH-TOPS)

NIGERSAURUS
(NEE-ZHAER-SORE-US)

WEIRD-AT-A-GLANCE

MAMENCHISAURUS
(MAH-MEHN-CHEE-SORE-US)

1

WEIRDEST HORNED DINO

The ceratopsian dinosaurs—four-legged herbivores with facial horns and neck frills—offer a lot to choose from in this category, but *Xenoceratops* is our winner. Though the first part of its name—"xeno"—means "alien," this late Cretaceous Canadian didn't earn its handle for its looks; the name is a nod to the shortage of horned dinosaur fossils where its remains were discovered.

2

WEIRDEST NECK

Eighty-two-foot (25-m)-long *Mamenchisaurus* had a neck that was almost half the length of its body! The late Jurassic sauropod could have swung its elongated neck side to side to chomp on vegetation over a wide area without ever moving its feet.

3

WEIRDEST-SHAPED HEAD

Nigersaurus's 500 teeth and wide, flat jaw were just right for scooping and slicing ground-level vegetation. The chompers were in comblike rows all the way at the front of its mouth, making the toothy portion of its skull wider than the rest!

MEGA MUNCHER

Nigersaurus's mouth has been called "vacuum-like" and "lawn-mower-like," and its munching has been compared to a cow's. Each of its tightly packed teeth was about the size of a toddler's incisor. Researchers who used a CAT scan (special type of x-ray) on a *Nigersaurus* skull found that there were nine replacement teeth stacked up behind each working tooth!

PTERODAUSTRO (TEH-ROE-DAW-STROH)

---

4 WEIRDEST SNACK

Paleontologists can usually tell from dinosaur fossils whether the animal ate plants or meat. But the skull of this parrot-beaked dino, along with the numerous gizzard stones found in its digestive tract, indicate that *Psittacosaurus* ate harder food such as seeds and nuts—offering the first firm evidence of a nut-eating dino.

5 WEIRDEST AMPHIBIAN

Beelzebufo weighed an estimated 10 pounds (4.5 kg) and was about as big as a beach ball. The immense amphibian—whose name means "devil toad"—lived on the island of Madagascar during the late Cretaceous and would have been big enough to be able to eat newly hatched dinos. *Ribbit!*

6 WEIRDEST TOOTHY BILL

Some pterosaurs had no teeth, while others had sharp teeth for spearing prey; *Pterodaustro*—which lived 100 million years ago in Argentina—had about 1,000 teeth in its long, pointy bill. Scientists think the needle-like teeth were used to scoop up and strain small crustaceans from the water. What a handy grill!

PSITTACOSAURUS (SIT-AH-CO-SORE-US)

BEELZEBUFO (BEE-ELL-ZEH-BOO-FOE)

WEIRDEST 117

BONEY
BLUNDERS

BRACHIOSAURUS SKELETON, BERLIN, GERMANY

There's no doubt paleontologists are supersmart, but nobody's perfect. Over the years, dinosaur scientists have made a lot of mistakes. That's how science works; you make a good guess about something, then test it to see if you're right. Others test it, too. And eventually you work the bugs out of the hypothesis and get closer and closer to the truth. But some of the mistakes scientists have made about dinosaurs have been especially bizarre. Here are a few of the weirdest:

Two Brains?: Scientists used to think that the lump on *Steyosaurus's* butt was a second brain (see page 61)! Now they think it may have been a place to store extra nutrients.

Diving Dino: Nineteenth-century paleontologists once believed that *Brachiosaurus* lived underwater, using its long neck as a snorkel to breathe, but later learned the behemoth lived on (and probably preferred mostly flat) land.

Thumbs Up (or Not): When Gideon Mantell identified *Iguanodon,* he put the plant-eater's thumb spike on its head.

Dino Hoax: Some scientists were very briefly duped in 1999 when a Chinese farmer combined skeletons from the front end of a primitive bird with the hind end of a dromaeosaur dinosaur, calling his creation *Archaeoraptor* and claiming it was the "missing link" between dinosaurs and birds. Since then, many genuine fossils of feathered dinosaurs with bird features have been found and described.

A STUDY FOUND THAT 48 PERCENT OF NEW DINOSAUR DISCOVERIES MADE BETWEEN 1850 AND 1980 HAD BEEN MISIDENTIFIED.

RIDDLE ME THIS!

Q: What do you get when you cross **a pig** with **a dinosaur?**

A: Jurassic Pork

Q: Why can't you hear **a pterosaur** in the bathroom?

A: Because the P is silent

Q: What do you get when **two dinosaurs** crash their cars?

A: Tyrannosaurus wrecks

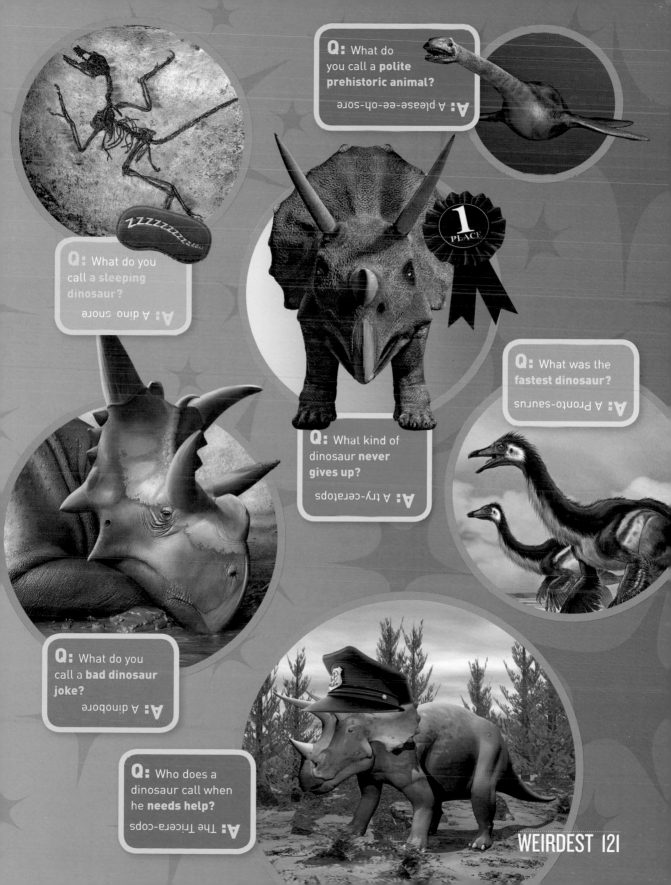

Q: What do you call a **polite prehistoric animal?**

A: A please-ee-oh-sore

Q: What do you call a **sleeping dinosaur?**

A: A dino snore

Q: What was the **fastest dinosaur?**

A: A Pronto-saurus

Q: What kind of dinosaur **never gives up?**

A: A try-ceratops

Q: What do you call a **bad dinosaur joke?**

A: A dinobore

Q: Who does a dinosaur call when he **needs help?**

A: The Tricera-cops

WEIRDEST 121

CHAPTER 5

DINOSAURS ARE SOME OF THE MOST INTRIGUING ANIMALS THAT EVER LIVED.

Dinos are cool for so many reasons that lots of them defy the usual record-breaking categories. To handle such an abundance of awesomeness, we created some new titles just for them! Turn the page to meet some of the most remarkable reptiles yet.

THE MOST FAMOUS DINOSAUR TYRANNOSAURUS REX
(TYE-RAN-OH-SORE-US RECKS)

T. rex may not have won the title of biggest or deadliest dino, but you knew this massive meat-eating king of the dinosaurs would take the crown for something. The hulking hunter-scavenger is arguably the most famous of all dinosaurs; it is a bona fide movie star, usually portrayed as a fierce, furious, unforgiving predator (and as a people-chaser, despite the approximately 60-million-year spread between *T. rex* and the earliest humans!). Its ferocious and famously powerful jaws contained 60 jagged teeth—the longest of which were longer than a dollar bill—suitable for crushing bones, tearing into the carcasses of other animals, and, occasionally, mugging for the camera.

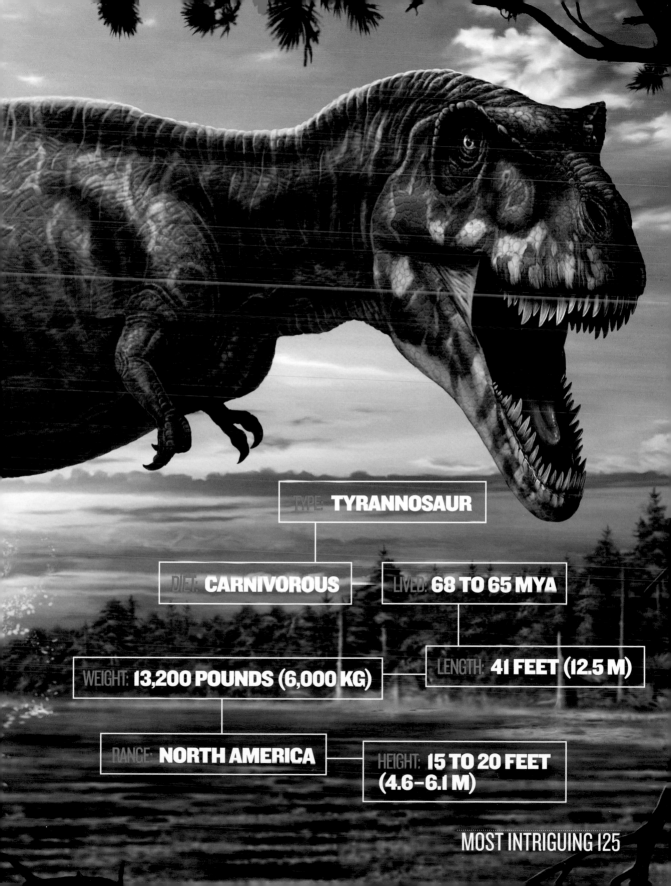

TYPE: TYRANNOSAUR

DIET: CARNIVOROUS

LIVED: 68 TO 65 MYA

WEIGHT: 13,200 POUNDS (6,000 KG)

LENGTH: 41 FEET (12.5 M)

RANGE: NORTH AMERICA

HEIGHT: 15 TO 20 FEET (4.6–6.1 M)

Check out some of the dinosaurs who made our most awesome list!

MOST ATTENTIVE MOTHER

MAIASAURA (MA-YA-SORE-A)

With a name that means "good mother lizard," you know *Maiasaura* had to be our winner. Scientists have found fossilized nests and eggshell fragments along-side the adult skeletons of these duck-billed dinos in "colonies," which suggests the late Cretaceous herbivores nested together in groups. The fossils of older juveniles found at these sites may mean that *Maiasaura* parents also took care of their young until they became independent, much like modern-day birds.

MOST **SOUTHERN DINO**

CRYOLOPHOSAURUS (CRY-OH-LOW-FO-SORE-US)

Dinosaurs have been found on every continent, including the coldest place on Earth: Antarctica. *Cryolophosaurus* roamed its forests—yes, forests!—190 million years ago, when the area was closer to the equator, and thus warmer, than it is now.

MOST **VALUABLE**

ARCHAEOPTERYX (ARK-EE-OP-TURR-ICKS)

Many fossil finds are valuable, but money isn't everything. The discovery of a 150-million-year-old *Archaeopteryx* fossil—first unearthed in the 19th century in Bavaria, southern Germany—is arguably the most important: Its bones show features of both reptiles and birds, making *Archaeopteryx* a "transitional fossil"— evidence that led scientists to the understanding that modern birds are actually the living descendants of dinosaurs. (Learn more about *Archaeopteryx* on pages 196–197.)

MOST **MAGICAL NAME**

DRACOREX HOGWARTSIA (DRAY-CO-REX HOG-WART-SEE-AH)

Harry Potter fans take note! The dino with the most magical moniker—*Dracorex hogwartsia*, or "Dragon King of Hogwarts"—is named after the famous fictional school of witchcraft and wizardry. Does this late Cretaceous pachycephalosaur with a knobbed, spiked head look like a dragon Harry and his friends might have encountered in their adventures? You decide, Muggle.

Meet more dinos with awesome attributes!

MOST **INTELLIGENT**

TROODON (TRO-OH-DON)

There is no way to know for sure which was the "smartest" dino. But *Troodon* is believed to have had the biggest brain-to-body ratio, which is a way scientists assess an animal's intelligence (see pages 50–51). The small, fast-running, late Cretaceous hunter had keen hearing and huge eyes that faced forward, allowing it to more accurately judge its distance from its prey before it attacked.

MOST TERRIFIC **TEETH**
EDMONTOSAURUS (ED-MON-TOH-SORE-US)

Edmontosaurus's wide snout was toothless (like a modern bird's beak), but its upper and lower jaws were packed with hundreds of small teeth; some *Edmontosaurus* skulls were found with more than 1,400 of them! Like other dinosaurs, below its visible teeth there were multiple replacement teeth at the ready. How cool is that? Duck-billed dino *Edmontosaurus* used its awesomely abundant teeth to grind up mouthfuls of plants in late Cretaceous North America.

MOST **MISNAMED**
OVIRAPTOR (OH-VIH-RAP-TORE)

Talk about a bad rap! *Oviraptor*—or "egg thief"—was uncovered next to a nest of eggs scientists believed belonged to another species of dino, leading them to believe *Oviraptor* was a nest raider. But researchers later discovered an oviraptorid baby inside one of the eggs, meaning the accused thief was probably the parent. *Oviraptor*-like skeletons have also been found sitting on top of a nest of eggs—much like modern birds do. Oops!

MOST **MENACING NECK**
SAUROPELTA (SORE-OH-PELT-AH)

Even Dracula would stay away from this gnarly neck! *Sauropelta*'s scruff and shoulders were dotted with intimidating-looking spikes, likely serving as a defense mechanism for the plant-eater as it walked the woodlands of early Cretaceous North America. The impressive ankylosaur (whose name means "shield lizard") was also covered along its back and long tail with bony plates, which could have offered it added protection from predators.

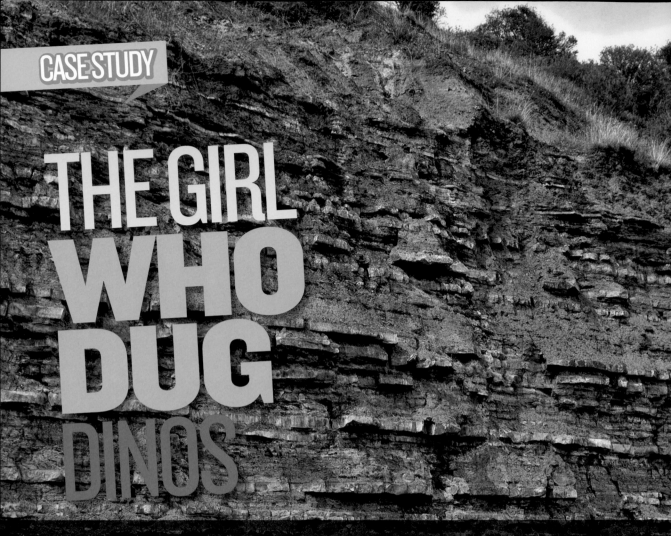

THE GIRL WHO DUG DINOS

At the beginning of the 19th century, when Mary Anning was a child in England, girls and women were discouraged from taking an interest in science—yet Mary defied the odds and became one of the most important paleontologists of her day. How? Her father enjoyed hunting fossils, and he taught Mary everything he knew. After Mary's father died when she was 11, Mary realized that she could help support her family by finding and selling fossils. Among her most significant discoveries were the first plesiosaur, the first complete ichthyosaur skeleton (and many more ichthyosaurs), and hundreds (maybe thousands) of other fossils—pretty fantastic finds for a person with no formal scientific training.

Not only did Mary find lots of fossils, but she also taught herself all about the field of paleontology. Her work became the basis of many other scientific developments. Her discoveries about geology and prehistoric life even helped scientists like Charles Darwin develop support for the theory of evolution! Although other scientists at the time respected Mary's work—often asking for her advice and opinions—she wasn't allowed to publish her findings under her own name because she was a woman and not wealthy. After her death, Mary's contributions to paleontology were mostly forgotten. But more recently people have begun to write books about her remarkable life and discoveries, finally giving superlative scientist Mary Anning the recognition she deserves.

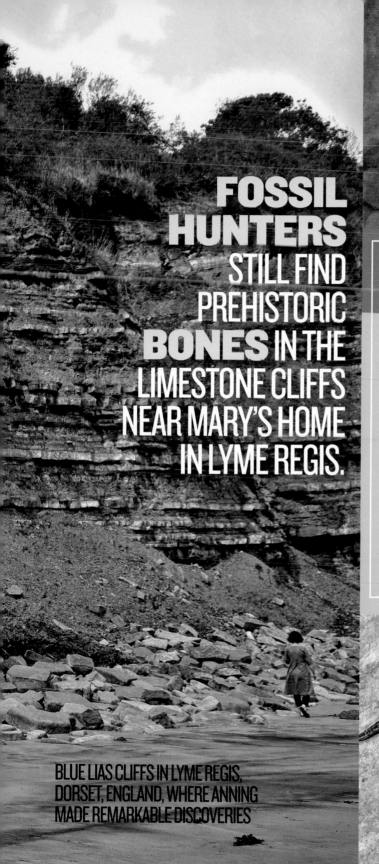

FOSSIL HUNTERS STILL FIND PREHISTORIC BONES IN THE LIMESTONE CLIFFS NEAR MARY'S HOME IN LYME REGIS.

BLUE LIAS CLIFFS IN LYME REGIS, DORSET, ENGLAND, WHERE ANNING MADE REMARKABLE DISCOVERIES

FINDS OF ALL KINDS

Mary Anning (1799–1847) made many important fossil finds, and her discoveries didn't stop at dinos. Her claims to fame include one of the first recognized pterosaur fossils and the fossil fish *Squaloraja*—which turned out to be a transitional form between sharks and rays. Mary figured this out by dissecting a modern ray and comparing it to the *Squaloraja* fossil. Whether she was digging up bones or dissecting specimens, Mary Anning didn't let other people's notions of what girls should or shouldn't do stop her from pursuing science—a lasting legacy, indeed!

FOSSIL OF A PTEROSAUR

REMARKABLE REPTILIANS IN ACTION!

Scientists have found fossils of dinosaurs and other prehistoric reptiles eating, fighting, and more! Here are just a few of their phenomenal finds.

TIMELESS TUSSLE: PROTOCERATOPS FIGHTING A VELOCIRAPTOR

DISCOVERED IN THE GOBI DESERT, MONGOLIA

A perfectly timed sand dune collapse (or sandstorm) uncovered one of the most famous dino fossils ever found. The 80-million-year-old battle scene features *Velociraptor*—a small but fierce predator—with its curved foot claw jammed into the neck of the plant-eating *Protoceratops*, which appears to have chomped down on *Velociraptor*'s right arm (and broken it) with its powerful mouth.

TRIPLE THREAT: FISH ENTANGLED WITH A PTEROSAUR THAT JUST ATE ANOTHER FISH
DISCOVERED IN SOLNHOFEN, GERMANY

The flying reptiles known as pterosaurs liked to hunt for fish, swooping down near the surface of the water and snatching them up in their beaks. But for the fossilized pterosaur called *Rhamphorhynchus*, this particular dive would be its last: As *Rhamphorhynchus* started to swallow its catch, the two-foot (60-cm)-long predatory fish *Aspidorhynchus* leapt out of the water and snagged the pterosaur's left wing with its pointy snout. Was *Aspidorhynchus* going for the same fishy prey as *Rhamphorhynchus*? Or for the pterosaur itself? Or was their collision just an unfortunate accident—a bad case of being in the wrong place at the wrong time? In the resulting struggle all three drowned (the small fish was still stuck in the pterosaur's throat!), sinking to the bottom of the lagoon until they were unearthed 155 million years later.

SMALL SNACK: SNAKE (NEARLY) EATING A BABY DINOSAUR
DISCOVERED IN GUJARAT, INDIA

It is rare to find a snake fossil, but to find one curled up with dinosaur eggs and about to devour a dino hatchling? That's sssssssuper rare! This 67-million-year-old fossil was the first ever evidence of snakes eating dinos. Scientists believe this species of snake could not open its mouth wide enough to eat dino eggs whole or break the shells, so it instead coiled up and waited patiently for its meal to emerge. Unfortunately for this 11.5-foot (3.5 m)-long slithering nest raider, a landslide interrupted its dinner.

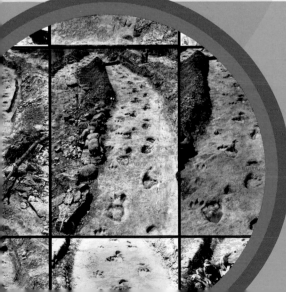

MAKING TRACKS: DINOSAURS ON THE MOVE
DISCOVERED IN GLEN ROSE, TEXAS, U.S.A.

About 110 million years ago, two dinos left their mark—literally—in an ancient North American riverbed. Preserved in rock, the footprints of a sauropod followed closely by those of a three-toed theropod seem to indicate the predator was in hot pursuit of the plant eater. Scientists have reconstructed the 147-foot (45-m) "chase" scene using a modern technology called photogrammetry, combining photographs to create a 3-D digital model of the track site.

MAKE UP YOUR
MIND, PLEASE

This mysterious dino has been subject to many misinterpretations over the years.

Stocky, 26-foot (7.9-m)-long *Plateosaurus* is one of the most studied—yet most puzzling—dinosaurs in Europe. It was named in 1837, and since then hundreds of skeletons of this hefty herbivore have been found in central and western Europe, many of them in Germany. When paleontologists first studied the bones of the late Triassic period plant-eater, which lived around 229 million to 200 million years ago, they thought it walked upright on two legs—only to decide later that it walked on all fours. A new thought is that it walked on two legs but with its back and tail held horizontal, instead of upright. Why so many changes? Because as more evidence emerges, and scientists spend time studying that evidence, they often discover new clues that make them change their minds. Scientists have had more than 179 years to study *Plateosaurus*, and during that time, their ideas about the big dino have changed a lot. And with new fossils being unearthed every year, there's no telling what changes they might discover next. (See pages 118–119 for some perplexing paleontological mix-ups.)

SCIENTISTS BELIEVE THAT THE PLANT-EATING PLATEOSAURUS **MOVED IN HERDS** AND MIGRATED TO FIND FOOD.

MOST DESERVING OF AN OSCAR

THE FIRST DEINONYCHUS REMAINS WERE FOUND IN 1931 IN MONTANA, U.S.A.

VELOCIRAPTOR

Filmmakers often change around facts to suit the story they are telling—especially when it comes to dinosaurs—that's one of the reasons they're so fun to watch. In the 1993 blockbuster film *Jurassic Park* there's one dino that really suffered a case of mistaken identity: the *Velociraptor.* Real *Velociraptors* (which lived during the Cretaceous period, not Jurassic) were one of the smallest of the raptor dinosaurs, only about the size of a poodle, and covered in feathers. In the movie, they stood six feet (1.8 meters) tall and had smooth, scaly skin! It turns out the *Velociraptors* in *Jurassic Park* were actually based on *Deinonychus,* an early Cretaceous period dino that stretched to more than 10 feet (3 m) long from head to tail, wielded wicked five-inch (12.7-cm) retractable claws on its feet, and most probably hunted in packs, like the *Velociraptors* in the film.

Jurassic Park did get some things right about *Velociraptor:* It was a vicious predator, with retractable hook-shaped claws on its feet (though its claws were only a mere three inches [7.6 cm]). But due to its diminutive size the *Velociraptor* likely preyed mostly on baby dinosaurs and small mammals, and only occasionally went for bigger prey. And although it was probably pretty smart, it may not have been clever enough to open doors—as it figured out how to do in the film, which won BIG with moviegoers. So this Oscar goes to ... *Deinonychus,* for portraying *Velociraptor* in the film *Jurassic Park!*

DEINONYCHUS HUNTED PREY MUCH LARGER THAN IT WAS.

DINO IQ

Troodon might have taken home top prize for most intelligent (pages 128–129), but check out how these other dinos might stack up in a battle of the brains.

DEINONYCHUS VS. IGUANODON

Dromaeosaurids (or raptors) like *Deinonychus* score pretty high when it comes to smarts (based on brain-to-body size ratios). And *Deinonychus* was probably sitting pretty at the top of the heap, easily trouncing most of the competition, including *Iguanodon*.

WINNER

ALLOSAURUS VS. HADROSAURUS

When it comes to smarts *Allosaurus* might not have been a match for *Troodon* and *Deinonychus*, but it was still one pretty sharp dino. It wins easily over *Hadrosaurus*, whose brain size was more like its close relative, *Iguanodon*—not tiny, but no prize winner either.

WINNER

WINNER

TRICERATOPS **VS.** STEGOSAURUS

No contest here! *Triceratops* might not have been the brightest bulb on the dino family tree, but it was probably smarter than *Stegosaurus*, which had a brain about the size of a lemon—in a body that could grow to almost 30 feet (9 m) long.

COMPSOGNATHUS **VS.** ORNITHOMIMUS

WINNER

Both were members of the dino honor society: the theropods. But even though *Ornithomimus* boasted a pretty large brain relative to its small body, *Compsognathus*'s more favorable brain-to-body ratio slightly edges him out for the win.

SKULLS AND BONES

Scientists name new dinosaur species at a pretty fast clip, but they're rarely lucky enough to find entire skeletons. Here are a few of the dinos for which we have found the most (relatively) complete skeletons.

100+ SKELETONS

PLATEOSAURUS
(PLAT-EE-OH-SORE-US)

12 SKELETONS

ARCHAEOPTERYX
(ARK-EE-OP-TURR-ICKS)

SUE, THE T. REX AT THE FIELD MUSEUM IN CHICAGO, ILLINOIS, U.S.A., IS THE **MOST COMPLETE** T. REX EVER FOUND.

DOZENS OF SKELETONS BUT ONLY 4 THAT ARE MORE THAN 48 PERCENT COMPLETE

100+ SKELETONS

TYRANNOSAURUS REX (TYE-RAN-OH-SORE-US RECKS)

PSITTACOSAURUS (SIT-AH-CO-SORE-US)

30 SKELETONS

IGUANODON (IG-WAN-OH-DON)

THE STURDY TURTLE

When you think of a rugged, resilient animal, you might not picture a turtle. But maybe you should! The 60- to 65-million-year-old remains of a North American river turtle show that the sturdy-shelled reptile survived the catastrophe that killed off the dinosaurs 65 million years ago. The discovery of *Boremys*, which had previously been known only from fossils that dated back to before that mass extinction, meant that the durable turtle must have survived the event that killed off a majority of Earth's plants and animals.

How could turtles have endured when countless others were lost forever? Researchers believe that it was not only living in the water that helped *Boremys* and other marine turtle species survive (while many land animals didn't) but also other adaptations that allowed it to hang tight in tough times: When conditions become difficult, aquatic turtles can slow down their metabolism and go several years without food or water, as well as dig and hunker down in mud holes. These amazing abilities likely came in handy for *Boremys* during and after the big event that made Earth uninhabitable for so many species. Talk about rolling with the punches!

TURTLES — GROUP: **REPTILES**

HABITAT: **OCEANS, PONDS, STREAMS, SWAMPS, FRESHWATER LAKES (AQUATIC TURTLES); GRASSLANDS, FORESTS, DESERTS (LAND TURTLES)**

NUMBER OF LIVING SPECIES: **ABOUT 300 CHELONIANS (TURTLES, TORTOISES, AND TERRAPINS)**

CURRENT RANGE: **WORLDWIDE, EXCEPT THE ARCTIC AND ANTARCTIC**

GET TO KNOW BOREMYS!

• *Boremys* feasted on crustaceans and soft plants in the North American lakes and streams where it lived.

• *Boremys* became extinct 42 million years ago and isn't closely related to any living turtle species.

• *Boremys* couldn't pull its head into its shell like modern turtles, so it was likely preyed upon to extinction by small mammals.

MOST-AT-A-GLANCE

REPENOMAMUS
(REH-PEEH-NO-MAY-MUSS)

THAT'S ONE BOLD BEAST

How do we know that *Repenomamus* was a dino-eater when many Mesozoic mammals stayed out of sight? It was reported in 2005 that the smaller of two *Repenomamus* fossils discovered in China—*Repenomamus robustus*—had been found with bones in its belly belonging to a baby *Psittacosaurus*, a plant-eating dinosaur that lived alongside the woodland-dwelling mammals 130 million years ago.

1 MOST AUDACIOUS MAMMAL

Most mammals that lived alongside the dinos posed little threat to even the smallest dinosaur. But strong-jawed, sharp-toothed *Repenomamus*—a predator that grew up to three feet (0.9 m) long and is possibly the biggest mammal of the Mesozoic era—was an exception: It hunted other vertebrates, including small dinosaurs!

2 MOST PECULIAR POSTERIOR

This pigeon-size dino could really shake its tail feathers! Tiny *Epidexipteryx* likely used its four bizarrely long back-end feathers for display or for balance as it scurried across tree branches in pursuit of insects in late Jurassic China.

3 MOST MILEAGE

Scientists believe that late Jurassic sauropod *Camarasaurus* migrated hundreds of miles seasonally—from lowlands to highlands and back again in what is now Utah and Wyoming, in the western United States. Why the long trip? To escape from droughts and head toward where food and water were plentiful.

EPIDEXIPTERYX
(EPP-IH-DEX-IPP-TEH-RIX)

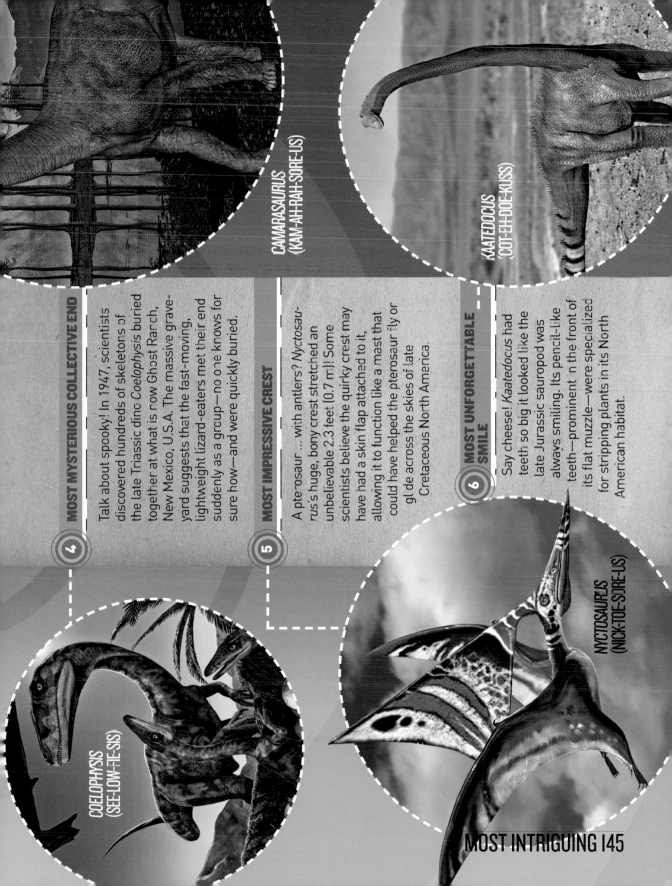

CAMARASAURUS
(KAM-AH-RAH-SORE-US)

KAATEDOCUS
(COT-EH-DOE-KUSS)

4 MOST MYSTERIOUS COLLECTIVE END

Talk about spooky! In 1947, scientists discovered hundreds of skeletons of the late Triassic dino *Coelophysis* buried together at what is now Ghost Ranch, New Mexico, U.S.A. The massive graveyard suggests that the fast-moving, lightweight lizard-eaters met their end suddenly as a group—no one knows for sure how—and were quickly buried.

5 MOST IMPRESSIVE CREST

A pterosaur ... with antlers? *Nyctosaurus*'s huge, bony crest stretched an unbelievable 2.3 feet (0.7 m)! Some scientists believe the quirky crest may have had a skin flap attached to it, allowing it to function like a mast that could have helped the pterosaur fly or glide across the skies of late Cretaceous North America.

6 MOST UNFORGETTABLE SMILE

Say cheese! *Kaatedocus* had teeth so big it looked like the late Jurassic sauropod was always smiling. Its pencil-like teeth—prominent in the front of its flat muzzle—were specialized for stripping plants in its North American habitat.

COELOPHYSIS
(SEE-LOW-FIE-SIS)

NYCTOSAURUS
(NICK-TOE-SORE-US)

THE FIRST TIME ANYONE SUGGESTED THAT MODERN BIRDS MIGHT BE DESCENDANTS OF DINOSAURS WAS IN THE MIDDLE OF THE 19TH CENTURY.

FLIGHT PLAN

One of the coolest things about dinosaurs is that you can hear their descendants singing outside your window early in the morning or see them gathering at your bird feeder when you leave for school. We know that birds evolved from carnivorous, two-legged dinos, but exactly how dinosaurs took to the air is one of the most perplexing dinosaur mysteries yet.

Some scientists think that birds evolved from dinosaurs that lived in trees and used their feathers to glide from branch to branch. This is known as the "top down" hypothesis. Other experts think that the "bottom up" hypothesis—in which dinosaurs that lived on the ground used the feathers on their forelimbs to catch a little air when they were chasing flying insects—might be closer to the truth. Which is right? The jury is still out, but you can be sure that scientists are working hard to figure out dinosaurs' flight plan.

ALTHOUGH MANY DINOSAURS DIDN'T USE THEIR FEATHERS TO FLY, THEY MAY HAVE USED THEM TO ATTRACT MATES AND TO KEEP THEIR BODIES—AND THEIR EGGS—WARM JUST LIKE MODERN BIRDS.

CLAIM TO

Connect these dinos with the distinction that landed them in our hall of records.

1 TROODON

2 NYCTOSAURUS

COELOPHYSIS

3

4 ARCHAEOPTERYX

A	**B**	**C**	**D**
MOST IMPRESSIVE CREST	MOST RELATIVELY COMPLETE SKELETONS FOUND	MOST FAMOUS	MOST INTELLIGENT

FAME

5 EDMONTOSAURUS

7 PLATEOSAURUS

8 CAMARASAURUS

6

TYRANNOSAURUS REX

E	F	G	H
MOST TEETH	MOST MILES TRAVELED	MOST VALUABLE	MOST DRAMATIC DEATH SCENE

CHAPTER 6

ROLL UP YOUR SLEEVES AND **DIG IN** TO THESE FANTASTIC **FIRSTS.**

The earliest dinosaurs started small and evolved during the Triassic period. They shared the land with insects and other invertebrates, prehistoric plants, small mammals, amphibians, and enormous, heavy reptiles like *Postosuchus*, a fierce, agile, sharp-toothed predator up to 15 feet (4.6 m) long and a distant cousin of modern crocs. Turn the page to step back—way back!—in time.

POSTOSUCHUS

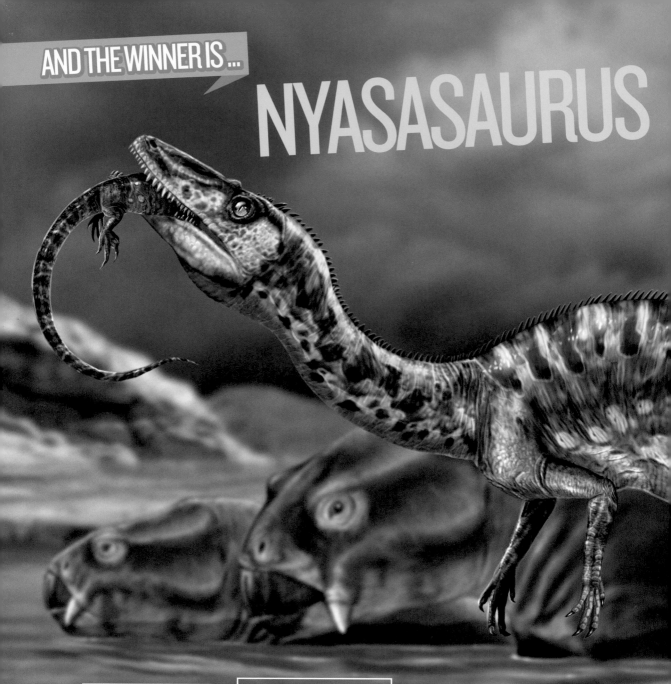

AND THE WINNER IS ...

NYASASAURUS

LIVED: ABOUT 240 MYA

LENGTH: 6.5 TO 10 FEET (2–3 M)

HEIGHT (AT THE HIP): 3 FEET (1 M)

RANGE: AFRICA

WEIGHT: 44 TO 132 POUNDS (20–60 KG)

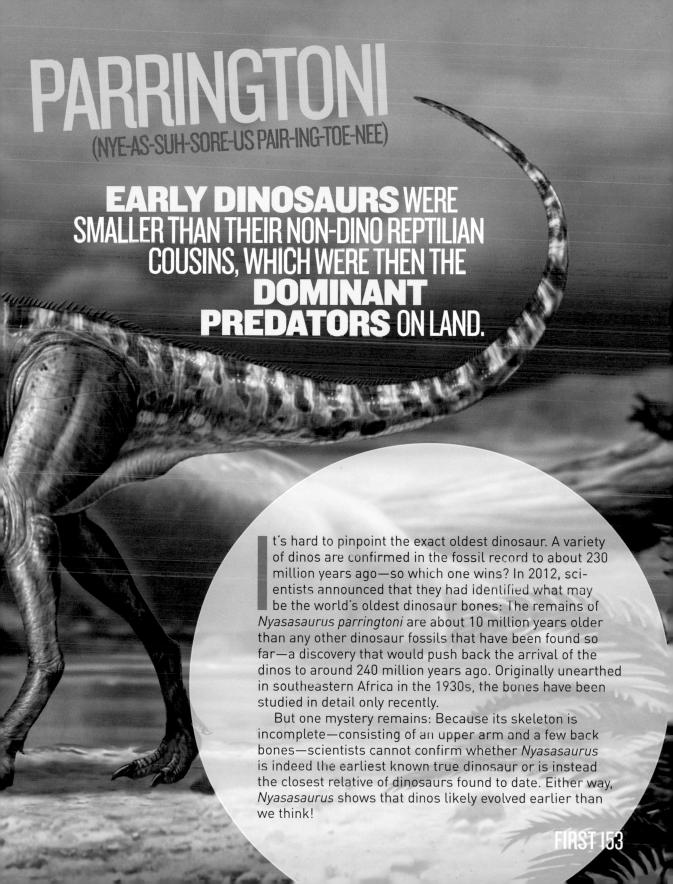

PARRINGTONI
(NYE-AS-SUH-SORE-US PAIR-ING-TOE-NEE)

EARLY DINOSAURS WERE SMALLER THAN THEIR NON-DINO REPTILIAN COUSINS, WHICH WERE THEN THE DOMINANT PREDATORS ON LAND.

It's hard to pinpoint the exact oldest dinosaur. A variety of dinos are confirmed in the fossil record to about 230 million years ago—so which one wins? In 2012, scientists announced that they had identified what may be the world's oldest dinosaur bones: The remains of *Nyasasaurus parringtoni* are about 10 million years older than any other dinosaur fossils that have been found so far—a discovery that would push back the arrival of the dinos to around 240 million years ago. Originally unearthed in southeastern Africa in the 1930s, the bones have been studied in detail only recently.

But one mystery remains: Because its skeleton is incomplete—consisting of an upper arm and a few back bones—scientists cannot confirm whether *Nyasasaurus* is indeed the earliest known true dinosaur or is instead the closest relative of dinosaurs found to date. Either way, *Nyasasaurus* shows that dinos likely evolved earlier than we think!

THE RUNNERS-UP ...

Time to turn back the clock to the Triassic! These pioneering dinos all date back to more than 200 million years ago.

HERRERASAURUS

(HUH-RARE-AH-SORE-US)

Herrerasaurus also inhabited South America approximately 228 million years ago, but it was bigger than *Eoraptor* (though still weighed only about as much as a lion). Believed by most experts to be one of the earliest theropods (predatory, two-legged dinos), *Herrerasaurus* was named after Victorino Herrera—the rancher in Argentina who discovered it.

Scientists have sometimes found it difficult to definitively classify Triassic period dinosaurs. They will start off believing a dino was an early type of sauropod, for example, and then—as they discover new fossil evidence, conduct new research, or perform further analysis—they reclassify it as an early theropod, or vice versa.

EORAPTOR
(EE-OH-RAP-TORE)

Eoraptor roamed river valleys in what is now Argentina about 228 million years ago. The sharp-toothed, fast-moving bipedal (two-legged) dinosaur was no longer than a major league baseball bat and only about the weight of a toddler. *Eoraptor* is thought to have preyed on lizards and other small reptiles, and some scientists believe it may also have eaten plants.

ISANOSAURUS
(IH-SAN-OH-SORE-US)

Late Triassic *Isanosaurus* was an early sauropod dinosaur, though—at about only 20 feet (6 m) long in adolescence—the woodland-dweller was much smaller than the giants that would come tens of millions of years later. Because the only remains of *Isanosaurus* found to date were not yet fully grown, scientists aren't sure exactly how big it could have gotten.

PLATEOSAURUS
(PLAT-EE-OH-SORE-US)

Plateosaurus was a plant-eater that roamed forests and swamps in what is now Europe between 216 and 204 million years ago. Discovered and named in the 1830s, *Plateosaurus* also stands out as one of the earliest dinosaurs recognized by science.

Explore some of the most excellent early happenings in dino history.

FIRST **FOSSILS**

ISCHIGUALASTO FORMATION

Some of the oldest known dinosaur remains have been discovered in rocks in northern Argentina, in an area known as Valley of the Moon. This lunar-looking landscape can be found in Ischigualasto Provincial Park, which, along with adjacent Talampaya National Park, contain the most complete continental fossil record of the beginnings of dinosaurs, mammals, and plants during the Triassic period.

FIRST USE OF THE TERM **DINOSAUR**

SIR RICHARD OWEN

We have 19th-century scientist Sir Richard Owen to thank for the term "dinosaur"—from the Greek words *deinos* ("fearfully great") and *sauros* (a lizard)—which he invented in 1842 to describe and group three of the earliest dino fossils ever discovered: mid-Jurassic predator *Megalosaurus*, early Cretaceous ankylosaur *Hylaeosaurus*, and early Cretaceous herbivore *Iguanodon*. (Owen knew they weren't lizards, but he chose the name because he thought they may have been related somehow.)

FIRST NEARLY COMPLETE DINO SKELETON **DISCOVERED**

HADROSAURUS (HAD-ROH-SORE-US)

The excavation of *Hadrosaurus* from a Haddonfield, New Jersey, U.S.A., pit in 1858, was a pretty big deal: Most of the dinosaur fossils found to that point had been fragments, and *Hadrosaurus* was an almost complete skeleton. What's even cooler is that its shorter front limbs proved for the first time that some dinosaurs walked on two legs! *Hadrosaurus* holds another honor: It's the official dinosaur of the state of New Jersey.

FIRST SCIENTIFICALLY DESCRIBED **DINO**

MEGALOSAURUS (MEG-AH-LOW-SORE-US)

All we know about dinosaurs began with a "great lizard": *Megalosaurus*, the first dinosaur fossil to be scientifically described (in 1824, by British geologist William Buckland). Remains of this mid-Jurassic predator had first been found in England in the 17th century, but at the time no one had ever heard of dinosaurs. The bones were thought possibly to have belonged to an elephant.

COLORFUL CREATURES

What's black and white and red all over? A dinosaur!

What color were dinosaurs? No one really knows. When artists paint pictures of dinosaurs (for books like this one!) or make models to display in museums, they have to guess what color the dinosaur might have been. To be on the safe side, they sometimes choose camouflage colors like green or brown or gray—which would have helped the giants blend into their surroundings. But that may all be about to change.

For the first time, scientists have found tiny bits of pigment—the chemicals that give animals and plants color—in dinosaur fossils. Found within microscopic organelles—called melanosomes—inside the dino's cells, the pigments are just like the ones in modern bird feathers ... and in your hair! Scientists have studied the pigments in a fossil of *Anchiornis*, a small, feathered dinosaur that lived during the Jurassic period in what is now China. They say that *Anchiornis* may have been colored a little bit like a woodpecker—black and white and red all over. It won't happen overnight, but once scientists analyze the pigments from other fossils, artists may know exactly which colors to use when they draw dinosaurs.

FLYING COLORS

Some scientists think dinosaurs were probably colored like modern birds: Males were brightly colored to attract mates, whereas females were kind of drab. Why don't females get to wear pretty colors, too? Mostly because they prefer to mate with flashy-looking males. The males with the brightest feathers get more mates and therefore make more baby birds, which, if they are males, inherit those flashier colors, leading to lots of brightly colored male birds. But there might be another reason as well. Dull-colored females may be less likely to attract predators to their nests while they are sitting on their eggs, so they produce more live babies and pass on to their daughters their seeming lack of fashion sense.

ANCHIORNIS

AWESOME ANCIENT ANIMALS

These cool creatures were around before—some way before!—the dinos.

TRILOBITES
(521 TO 250 MYA)

WHAT THEY ARE: One of the earliest known groups of arthropods, a group of invertebrates that includes the insects, crustaceans, myriapods (centipedes, millipedes), and arachnids that scamper across Earth today.

WHY THEY ARE AWESOME: The remains of tiny trilobites are abundant and have been found all over the world. These little critters evolved into thousands of known species and dominated the oceans for more than a quarter billion years.

OPABINIA (510 TO 500 MYA)

WHAT IT IS: This quirky, five-eyed creature is so outside-the-box it doesn't fit into any one animal group. But because it does share some traits with arthropods, scientists think it might be related to an arthropod ancestor.

WHY IT IS AWESOME: The 2.5-inch (6.5-cm) aquatic oddity probably used the grasping claws at the end of its inch-long (0.3-cm) flexible trunklike appendage— or proboscis—to grab prey and stuff it into its mouth.

EURYPTERIDS
(470 TO 248 MYA)

WHAT THEY ARE: Among the first and most ferocious aquatic predators and the largest arthropods ever to have existed.

WHY THEY ARE AWESOME: Some measuring longer than an adult human, these giant scorpion-like animals trolled prehistoric waters for slow-moving snacks. Some may have even been able to crawl on land for a short distance!

DUNKLEOSTEUS
(380 TO 360 MYA)

WHAT THEY ARE: Armored fish covered with bony plates up to two inches (5 cm) thick and one of the earliest "jawed" fishes.

WHY THEY ARE AWESOME: About 33 feet (10 m) long with bladed jaws instead of teeth, this prehistoric predator had a bite force scientists believe was the strongest of any fish ever. It also could open its mouth in one-fiftieth of a second—a speed that would have caused a suction powerful enough to pull its prey directly into its mouth.

NAUTILOIDS
(500 MYA TO THE PRESENT)

WHAT THEY ARE: Shelled sea-dwellers and the earliest of the cephalopods, a group of animals that also includes squids and octopuses.

WHY THEY ARE AWESOME: Nautiluses have remained mostly unchanged for millions of years. In prehistoric times, there were about 10,000 different species of nautiloid, but only a few species—including the chambered nautilus—survive today.

ANCIENT PEOPLE MAY HAVE SEEN AN **ELEPHANT FOSSIL** AND MISTAKEN THE CENTER HOLE WHERE THE TRUNK COMES OUT FOR AN **EYEHOLE**, LEADING TO THE MYTH OF THE CYCLOPS.

STATUE OF THE HERO HERCULES WRESTLING WITH A SEA MONSTER, SUFFOLK, ENGLAND

MYTHS AND MONSTERS, OH MY!

Since the first dinosaur was described in the 19th century, the larger-than-life lizards have caused people's imaginations to run wild with tales of what the animals and their ancient worlds looked like. But it turns out the prehistoric wonders may have been inspiring epic stories long before anyone knew what they were.

Ancient Greeks, for example, were some of the most prolific storytellers in history, creating many myths, legends, and lore that include fantastical creatures like giants, monsters, and dragons—but the ancient people who made up these myths may have been inspired by fossils. Scientists learned that the islands where many of these myths originated are rich in fossils, and the people of ancient Greece and Rome collected and displayed them, much like museums do today. Ancient Greeks and Romans didn't have enough scientific knowledge to learn much about the animals the bones came from, but they probably did understand that the petrified bones were relics from earlier times. Adrienne Mayor, a scholar who studies the myths of ancient Greece and Rome, believes they used those fossils to support their traditional stories—or to inspire new ones.

ANCIENT INSPIRATION

- The gigantic sea monster that Greek god Poseidon sent to terrorize the city of Troy (after the king refused to pay the sea god for building the city's walls) may have been inspired by a skull of an extinct giraffe. Many fossils like this have been found on the Greek islands. Not to worry, though. The hero Heracles killed the sea monster and saved the day!
- Mastodon fossils found on the Greek isle of Samos were possibly thought to be the bones of the giant war elephants Dionysus—god of nature and wine—used in his bloody battle with the female warriors called Amazons.
- Long-extinct mammal bones may have inspired ancient Greeks to believe that giant humans or gods—like Ares (god of war), Hades (god of the underworld), and Aphrodite (goddess of love and beauty)—had once walked the Earth.
- Other fossils found on the Greek isle of Samos were the likely inspiration for the mythological beasts called Neades. These monstrous, terrifying animals were said to have roamed the island and were capable of "splitting the land" with a single roar.

DRACORAPTOR

A NEW DRAGON IN TOWN

Move over *Dracorex hogwartsia*, there's a new dragon in town! It may not sport a fancy name inspired by a blockbuster book and movie series (see pages 126–127), but *Dracoraptor* (which means "dragon thief") was equally impressive. Discovered in 2014 near Cardiff, Wales, and named in 2016, it is one of the first nearly complete skeletons from the early Jurassic period found so far. *Dracoraptor* is an important discovery, because it lived when dinosaurs were first starting down the evolutionary path that led to the big carnivores of the Cretaceous, dinosaurs like *T. rex* and *Velociraptor*.

The *Dracoraptor* this fossil is from was not quite fully grown. It was about six and a half feet (2 m) long, with short arms and big hands. It could move fast and had sharp teeth to tear into the meat of the prey it caught. By studying *Dracoraptor*, scientists will be able to learn more about how dinosaurs evolved and came to dominate the planet after the major extinction at the end of the Triassic period. That extinction wiped out about 76 percent of the species on Earth, including a lot of dinosaurs, but paved the way for many other dinos that flourished during the Jurassic period, including *Dracoraptor*.

WALES, THE COUNTRY WHERE DRACORAPTOR WAS DISCOVERED, HAS A DRAGON ON ITS FLAG.

WHO CAME FIRST?

The Age of Dinosaurs lasted for more than 160 million years and covered three different geological periods: Triassic, Jurassic, and Cretaceous. Find out which of these dinos takes the honors for coming in first in its period.

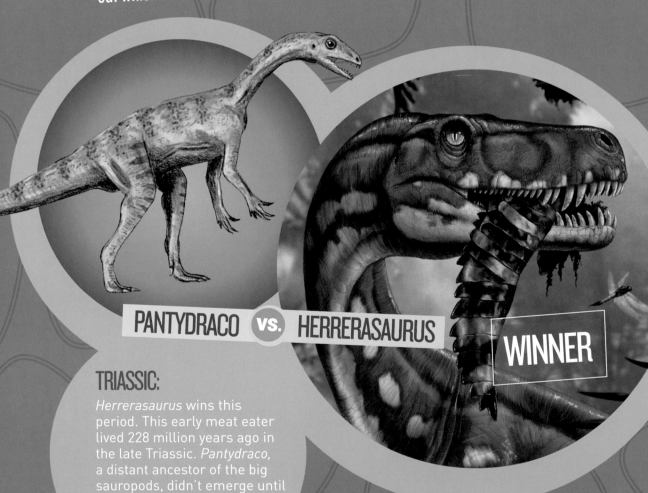

PANTYDRACO VS. HERRERASAURUS

WINNER

TRIASSIC:

Herrerasaurus wins this period. This early meat eater lived 228 million years ago in the late Triassic. *Pantydraco*, a distant ancestor of the big sauropods, didn't emerge until around 25 million years later.

MEGAPNOSAURUS VS. ALLOSAURUS

WINNER

JURASSIC:

Megapnosaurus—a feathered theropod and close relative of *Coelophysis*—lived in the early Jurassic, about 199 million years ago, whereas the tardy *Allosaurus* showed up with its knifelike teeth and wicked claws only around 150 million years ago, during the late Jurassic.

APPALACHIOSAURUS VS. PSITTACOSAURUS

CRETACEOUS:

Drumroll, please: The winner is *Psittacosaurus!* This parrot-beaked herbivore lived 125 million years ago in the early Cretaceous. *Appalachiosaurus* (for which scientists found a near complete skeleton in the Appalachian mountains of Alabama) on the other hand, didn't arrive until about 77 million years ago.

WINNER

MEGA MILESTONES

The history of Earth goes back a loooong way.
Check out some of the most magnificent milestones!

200,000

years ago:
Homo sapiens

210

million years
ago: **Early
mammals**

4.6
billion years ago:
Earth formed

543
million years ago:
mollusks, hydras, sponges, echinoderms, trilobites

THE SUPER OCEAN THAT SURROUNDED THE SUPERCONTINENT **PANGAEA** WAS CALLED **PANTHALASSA.**

530
million years ago:
First animals with backbones

200
million years ago: Pangaea begins to break up

230
million years ago: **Early dinosaurs**

SUPER SURVIVORS

There's no debating that sponges (poriferans) were among the first animals on Earth, but scientists have for years disagreed on exactly *when* these curious creatures first appeared.

In 2015, a team of researchers identified something in a geologic formation in southern China that helped pin down the date: a well-preserved 600-million-year-old sponge, only around .04 inch (1 mm) in height and width. Even more intriguing, in 2016, scientists found a molecule likely belonging to a sea sponge in 640-million-year-old rocks—a "molecular fossil" that could very well make the sea sponge the oldest animal on Earth!

Why is getting the right date so important? Scientists believe that the split between sponges and most other animals was a significant event in the early history of life on Earth. Pinpointing that split helps us better understand the timing and process of animal evolution. Just goes to show: A small find can be a very big deal!

IT'S A WHAT?!?

Sponges resemble a lot of familiar things: branches, tubes, bushes, and balls, to name just a few. But do they look like any *animals* you can think of? Likely not! Sponges have no muscles, no circulatory system, no nervous system, and no internal organs, but they are indeed animals. Sponges are very diverse and come in a large variety of shapes and colors; they can be found in waters worldwide—from the tropics to polar regions—and are serious supersurvivors: There have been five mass extinctions in Earth's history, and sponges have endured them all.

VASE SPONGE

TUBE SPONGE

GROUP: **INVERTEBRATES**

CURRENT RANGE: **WORLDWIDE**

HABITAT: **MOSTLY IN SALTWATER; SOME DWELL IN FRESHWATER**

NUMBER OF LIVING SPECIES: **9,000 OR MORE**

THAT FAMILIAR SPONGE ON YOUR KITCHEN SINK **WASN'T PLUCKED FROM THE OCEAN!** MOST HOUSEHOLD SPONGES ARE **HUMAN-MADE** USING PLANT FIBERS (CELLULOSE) AND CHEMICALS.

FIRST-AT-A-GLANCE

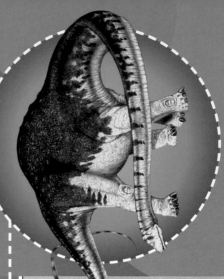

COELOPHYSIS
(SEE-LOW-FIE-SIS)

HYPSELOSAURUS
(HIP-SELL-OH-SORE-US)

1 FIRST DINOS IN SPACE

Think dinos are out of this world? You're right! Bones and eggshells belonging to *Maiasaura* accompanied astronaut Loren Acton on his mission to *SpaceLab 2* in 1985. Thirteen years later, a 210-million-year-old skull belonging to *Coelophysis* was aboard the shuttle *Endeavour* as it made its way toward the Mir space station.

2 FIRST DINO FOUND IN BIRDLIKE SLEEPING POSE

Aw! *Mei long* (whose name means "soundly sleeping dragon") was the first dinosaur fossil to have been found in a sleeping pose—with its face tucked in behind a front limb—similar to that displayed by resting and sleeping modern-day birds. Time to catch some z's.

3 FIRST DINO EGGS DISCOVERED

A Roman Catholic priest named Jean-Jacques Pouech is credited as being the first person to discover dinosaur eggs. He uncovered the shell fragments in southern France in 1859, describing them as "enormous eggshells, at least four times the volume of ostrich eggs." He had no idea they belonged to the late Cretaceous sauropod *Hypselosaurus*!

MEI LONG (MAY LONG)

PTERODACTYLUS
(TEH-ROE-DACK-TILL-US)

4. FIRST TURTLE WITH FULLY FORMED SHELL

The first turtle to have a complete, top-and-bottom shell (like today's turtles), *Proganochelys* dates back to the late Triassic. Though it looks much like modern turtles, the prehistoric reptile had spikes on its neck and tail and could not retract its head into its shell.

5. FIRST SEEDS OF FLOWERING PLANTS

Flowers seem to be everywhere, but they haven't always been! It actually wasn't until the Cretaceous period that the earliest flowering plants evolved. The oldest known seeds of angio-sperms (flowering plants) date back 125 million to 110 million years and were no bigger than 0.1 inch (2.5 mm) wide. Some scientists believe there is fossil evidence dating the first flowering plants back to the Jurassic period, but this is still controversial.

6. FIRST PTEROSAUR FOUND

When Cosimo Collini discovered *Pterodactylus* way back in 1784, he had no idea he was the first to uncover a flying reptile; the Italian naturalist thought the winged creature used its large arms to paddle in the sea. *Pterodactylus* dates to 150 to 144 million years ago, when it hunted for small fish in coastal areas of what is now Germany.

PROGANOCHELYS
(PRO-GAN-OH-KELL-ISS)

BOTTOM TO TOP

Odontochelys swam around shallow coastal waters about 220 million years ago, around ten million years before *Proganochelys*. Though it did have a plastron (the flat under-side of a shell), it did not have a carapace (a shell on its back)—likely meaning turtle shells began forming underneath first, only later expanding and growing together at the top to make the fully formed shell we see today.

BLOODY BONES REVEAL A MAJOR DISCOVERY

Most of what we know about dinosaurs we learn from their bones. That's because the hard parts of animals, like bones, gradually absorb minerals from their surroundings and after a long time turn into fossils. The soft parts, like skin and blood, usually just decay, or dissolve away. But even though the softer parts don't fossilize, they can sometimes survive for a very long time. Recently, scientists used a modern technique called mass spectrometry to analyze the chemicals in 80-million-year-old hadrosaur fossils—and they made a major discovery: They found cells that lined the walls of the dinosaur's blood vessels.

It's supercool to be able to look at the blood vessel cells of a long-extinct dinosaur, but this discovery is useful, too. Studying red blood cells will help scientists better understand when the modern birds we know today evolved from their ancient reptile ancestors, the dinosaurs.

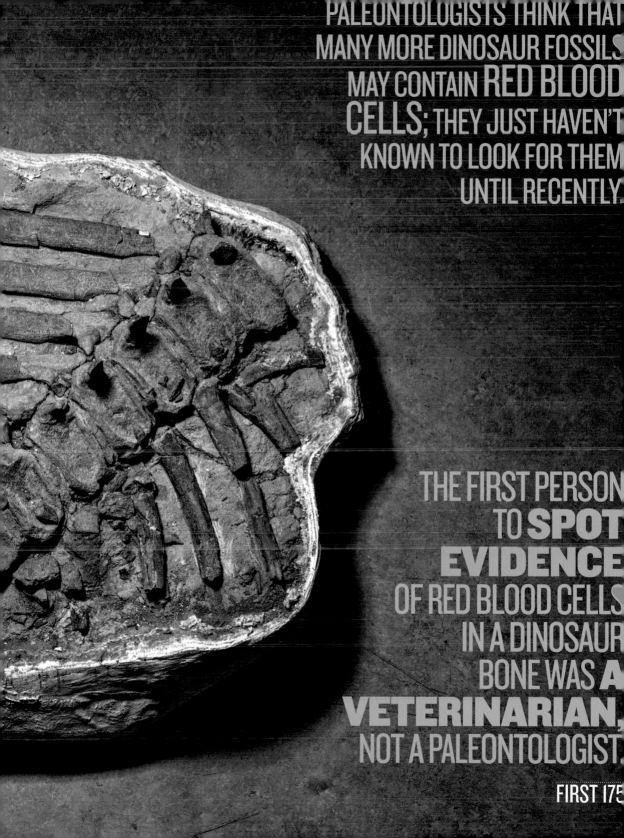

PALEONTOLOGISTS THINK THAT MANY MORE DINOSAUR FOSSILS MAY CONTAIN **RED BLOOD CELLS**; THEY JUST HAVEN'T KNOWN TO LOOK FOR THEM UNTIL RECENTLY.

THE FIRST PERSON TO **SPOT EVIDENCE** OF RED BLOOD CELLS IN A DINOSAUR BONE WAS **A VETERINARIAN**, NOT A PALEONTOLOGIST.

NAME THAT DINO!

Test your knowledge of some famous dino firsts found in this chapter.

I. WHAT IS THE OLDEST DINOSAUR FOUND TO DATE?
A. *Nyasasaurus*
B. *Utahraptor*
C. *Appalachiosaurus*

2. WHAT WAS THE EARLIEST OF THE BIG PREDATORY DINOS?
A. *Herrerasaurus*
B. *Carnotaurus*
C. *Giganotosaurus*

3. WHAT WAS THE FIRST NEARLY COMPLETE DINO SKELETON EVER FOUND?
A. *Tyrannosaurus rex*
B. *Hadrosaurus*
C. *Triceratops*

176

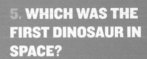

4. NAME THE FIRST DINO TO BE SCIENTIFICALLY DESCRIBED.
A. *Diplodocus*
B. *Apatosaurus*
C. *Megalosaurus*

5. WHICH WAS THE FIRST DINOSAUR IN SPACE?
A. *Archaeopteryx*
B. *Maiasaura*
C. *Edmontosaurus*

6. WHICH WAS THE FIRST DINOSAUR FOUND IN A BIRDLIKE SLEEPING POSE?
A. *Mussaurus*
B. *Yinlong*
C. *Mei long*

CHAPTER 7

THE DEMISE OF THE DINOS MADE WAY FOR NEW AMAZING (AND RECORD-BREAKING!) PREHISTORIC ANIMALS.

Earth's first mammals evolved at the same time as the first dinosaurs and coexisted alongside the giant reptiles for millions of years. Though mammals were already becoming more diverse during the Cretaceous period, it was the cataclysmic occurrence that doomed the dinos about 65 million years ago that allowed them to evolve into a bigger, deadlier, weirder, and even more diverse group. The Age of Dinosaurs had ended, and the Age of Mammals had begun.

MAMMOTH

Also surviving the mass extinction at the end of the Cretaceous period were plenty of non-dino reptiles—including crocodiles, snakes, and lizards—as well as birds and smaller amphibians. But, outcompeted by mammals, they never came to dominate the land as the dinosaurs had.

PARACERATHERIUM
(PARRA-SERRA-THEER-EE-UM)

DIET: HERBIVOROUS

RANGE: ASIA

LIVED: BETWEEN ABOUT 35 AND 20 MYA

WEIGHT: 16 TO 22 TONS (15–20 T)

LENGTH: 26 FEET (8 M)

HEIGHT (AT SHOULDER): 18.25 FEET (5.5 M)

PARACERATHERIUM WAS AS TALL AT ITS SHOULDER AS THE WORLD'S TALLEST MODERN-DAY MAMMAL— THE GIRAFFE— IS AT THE TOP OF ITS HEAD.

Over the course of millions of years, mammals grew to be the dominant animals on land—even rivaling the staggering size of some of their reptilian predecessors. This hornless early rhino known as *Paraceratherium*—sometimes called *Indricotherium* or *Baluchitherium*—is thought to have been the largest land mammal ever to have lived. Three times as heavy as *T. rex*, its skull alone was a whopping 4.25 feet (1.3 m) long—probably about as big as you! Its huge body and superlong neck allowed it to munch much like a present-day giraffe does, feeding on leaves at the tops of trees as it roamed areas of present-day Asia, including Mongolia and China.

Huge, deadly, and weird didn't end with the extinction of the dinosaurs! Check out some of the record breakers that came next.

DEADLIEST SHARK

MEGALODON (MEG-AH-LOW-DON)

Even Jaws would have been no match for this formidable fish! *Carcharodon megalodon*—which swam in Earth's ocean 16 million years ago—was the largest predatory shark that ever lived. Stretching about four times as long and 20 times as heavy as today's great white sharks, *C. megalodon* had long, serrated (sawlike) triangular teeth suitable for shredding prey, including seals, dolphins, whales, and turtles. Its bite was up to 10 times stronger than a great white's!

BIGGEST **SLOTH**
MEGATHERIUM (MEG-AH-THEE-REE-UM)

Is that a supersized bear? Not quite! The largest known ground sloth, *Megatherium*—meaning "great beast"—roamed woodlands of the Americas until about 10,000 years ago. Covered with long, thick hair, this 20-foot (6-m)-long, 4.4-ton (4-t) mammal could rest its significant girth on its powerful hind legs, using its tail for balance and its massive claws to grab branches and munch on leaves and grasses.

MOST MASSIVE **SNAKE**
TITANOBOA (TY-TAN-O-BO-AH)

At around 48 feet (14.6 m) long and weighing more than a ton, *Titanoboa* is thought to have been the biggest snake of all time. This spectacular serpent, which slithered through South American swamps 60 to 58 million years ago hunting fish and other reptiles— including ancient crocodiles!—was much longer and heavier than today's largest living snakes, which don't even come close to its stupendous size.

WEIRDEST **ANIMAL**
MACRAUCHENIA (MACK-ROW-KAY-NEE-AH)

It's the ultimate animal mash-up! Dating back seven million years, this 10-foot (3-m)-long, 1,550-pound (700-kg) plant-eater had the small head and long neck of a camel, three-toed feet like a rhino, and openings for its nostrils on top of its head, like a whale. It also had an extremely curious nose: a long, flexible trunk that looks a bit like an elephant's, only shorter.

MORE RUNNERS-UP ...

Explore more extreme animals that dominated after the dinos!

SMALLEST HORNED MAMMAL

CERATOGAULUS (SEH-RAT-O-GOW-LUS)

At only a foot (0.3 m) long and less than 10 pounds (4.5 kg), *Ceratogaulus* was the smallest known mammal with horns. (Mammals with horns today include bison, antelope, and rhinos.) It's thought that the pint-size rodent—which lived in North American woodlands 10 to 5 million years ago—may have used the two horns above its tiny nose to defend itself when it left its burrow to forage.

DEADLIEST FELINE

SMILODON (SMYL-O-DON)

This 880-pound (400-kg) carnivorous cat was the *purr-r*fect predator. Its sharp, serrated teeth were just right for slicing open the horses, bison, deer, and mammoths that shared its North and South American habitat between 2.5 million and 10,000 years ago. *Smilodon* is thought to have been able to open its jaw more than 120 degrees—wide enough to sink its long, curvy canines into its massive prey.

CROCODYLUS (CROC-OH-DIL-US)

Though there's no direct evidence that this prehistoric predator ate our human ancestors, scientists believe it's definitely possible. This 27-foot (8.3-m)-long reptile lurked near the lakes where early humans would have collected water, so the considerable croc could have—gulp—ambushed them there and swallowed them whole. *Crocodylus thorbjarnarsoni*—which inhabited present-day Kenya between four and two million years ago—was so huge it took four people to lift just one fossilized skull!

MOST MASSIVE FLYING BIRD

ARGENTAVIS (ARE-JEN-TAY-VISS)

Scientists believe this immense bird of prey weighing upward of 176 pounds (80 kg) more likely glided than flew; *Argentavis* was so heavy that instead of flapping its wings to take off it probably ran downhill into a head-wind (like a human hang glider) to become airborne. This beaked scavenger—with a wingspan of about 20 feet (6 m)—swooped down on dead meat it spotted from the air about six million years ago.

A MAMMOTH MYSTERY

We know exactly what woolly mammoths looked like because during the last ice age some of them were frozen solid in ice! They had a heavy coat of fur and a thick layer of fat to help them survive in subzero temperatures. The massive mammals were so well adapted to living in extreme cold that a warming climate may have helped cause their extinction. Or was it the other way around? Did the extinction of the mammoths help make the planet warmer?

Consider this: Woolly mammoths grazed and pooped on grasslands in the cold, dry northern plains where they lived. Their droppings fertilized and kept the grasslands healthy. Underneath the grass was a permanently frozen layer of earth, something called permafrost, that trapped even more carbon than all of the world's rain forests do

WHAT'S THE BIG DEAL WITH CARBON, ANYWAY?

Carbon is an element, like oxygen and hydrogen, and it is everywhere—it's the fourth most common element in the universe. On Earth, carbon is stored in rocks, oceans, plants, and soil. When carbon is released into the atmosphere, it causes the temperature of Earth to rise. Over long spans of time, Earth keeps a balance between how much carbon is stored and how much is released. But sometimes things like melting permafrost or burning fossil fuels can release a lot of carbon in the atmosphere in a relatively short period of time, increasing temperatures quickly and causing dramatic changes in Earth's environments.

today. When the mammoths were no longer around to keep the grasslands healthy, the permafrost lost its insulation and began to melt. This released carbon back into the atmosphere and helped make the planet even warmer. So global warming might have finished off the woolly mammoths—but finishing off the mammoths only made global warming worse.

LOOK FAMILIAR? WOOLLY MAMMOTHS AND MODERN-DAY ELEPHANTS SHARE A COMMON ANCESTOR.

PREHISTORIC ANIMALS 187

You might recognize a few of these creatures—and merely marvel at the others! Check out these amazing early relatives of animals in our world today.

IT'S ALL RELATIVE

WALKING WHALE

NAME: *AMBULOCETUS*
(AM-BYOO-LOW-SEE-TUSS)
SIZE: 9.75 feet (3 m) long
DATES FROM: About 50 million years ago
FOSSILS FOUND: Pakistan
FANTASTIC FACTS: This early member of the whale family had four legs and could walk on land—really! But with flipperlike back feet, the 400-pound (180-kg) mammal was probably more of a waddler than a sprinter. Its hunting style may have been to ambush prey near the shallow seas and rivers where it lived and swam. *Ambulocetus* is a "transitional fossil"—one that shows us how whales were once land mammals that made their way into the sea ... and stayed there.

GOING BATTY

NAME: *ICARONYCTERIS*
(ICK-AH-ROE-NICK-TEH-RISS)
SIZE: 5.5 inches (14 cm) long
DATES FROM: About 52 million years ago
FOSSILS FOUND: Wyoming, U.S.A.
FANTASTIC FACTS: One of the earliest types of bats ever found to date, *Icaronycteris* was a tiny night flier with a long tail and a funky claw sticking out from its wings. Like modern-day bats, this insect-eater used echolocation (sound waves and echoes) to find its prey.

ARMORED VEHICLE
NAME: *GLYPTODON* (GLIP-TOE-DON)
SIZE: 6.5 to 8.25 feet (2–2.5 m)
DATES FROM: 2 million to 10,000 years ago
FOSSILS FOUND: North and South America
FANTASTIC FACTS: This early armadillo-like animal was covered in more than 1,000 small bony tiles (or osteoderms)—each about one inch (2.5 cm) thick—over its domed back and its tail, which would have protected it against predators.

A HORSE, OF COURSE
NAME: *MERYCHIPPUS* (MEH-REE-CHIP-US)
SIZE: 3.5 feet (1.1 m) tall
DATES FROM: About 17-10 million years ago
FOSSILS FOUND: U.S.A. and Mexico
FANTASTIC FACTS: Though not the first ever horse, *Merychippus* was more like modern horses than those that came before. Larger, faster, and with a longer muzzle than its forest-dwelling, leaf-eating ancestors, this early equine lived on plains in large herds and is thought to be the first horse that fed exclusively on grass.

EXTINCTION: WHAT

More than 90 percent of all the plants and animals that have ever lived are now extinct. When an animal disappears from Earth, other animals that had competed with it for food or places to live—or that might have been eaten by it—now have room not only to survive but also to thrive. A mass extinction that wipes out half or more living species allows the opportunity for lots of new ones to evolve and spread across the planet.

The biggest extinction event in the history of Earth was the Permian-Triassic (approximately 251 million years ago), which paved the way for the dinosaurs to dominate the Mesozoic era. Then, around 65 million years ago, another extinction did in the dinosaurs, making way for new plants and animals to flourish. Had dinosaurs not died off, humans might never have had the opportunity to evolve. But many scientists believe that if humans continue to pollute the environment, clear forests, and overfish the oceans, half of Earth's current species may be driven to extinction by the next century. Because humans depend on forests and oceans and many modern animals to survive, it's in our interest to practice conservation—and to keep our planet a habitable spot for humans!

AN ARTIST IMAGINES THE ASTEROID THAT DOOMED THE DINOS.

COMES NEXT?

THE PERMIAN-TRIASSIC EXTINCTION WIPED OUT ABOUT 90 PERCENT OF MARINE SPECIES AND 70 PERCENT OF LAND ANIMALS.

KILLER PIG

Make no bones about it, entelodonts were pretty bad dudes—so bad that the name entelodont doesn't do them justice. These vicious killing machines were so fearsome that they earned themselves the nickname "Terminator Pig." Probably closer relatives of modern hippos than of actual pigs, entelodonts lived between 49 and 37 million years ago during the middle of the Miocene period. The supersized omnivores were scavengers; they had extremely powerful jaws and ate just about anything they wanted, including the early ancestors of rhinos and camels. Their massive teeth and enormous tusks would have made killing prey a breeze, even though they probably weren't very fast.

The behemoths were brawlers—even with their own kind. Paleontologists have found entelodont skulls with deep gashes made by other entelodonts. The bite marks on some fossils show that these prehistoric pigs would often grab the entire snout of another entelodont in their mouths, ripping each other open and crushing their relatives' skulls in their powerful jaws, taking family fights to extremes.

ENTELODONTS FACE OFF.

PALEONTOLOGISTS
FOUND A PILE OF SMALL
PREHISTORIC CAMELS
THAT HAD BEEN BITTEN IN
HALF BY ENTELODONTS.

ON THE HUNT

Many dinos were master hunters, but the animals who came after them also possessed some superlative skills. Check out who we think might have won our imagined matchups.

WINNER

Albertosaurus was a terror on land, but it is likely that at least some of the time it depended on its pack mates to help take down its prey. *Megalodon* gets the cup because it probably terrorized the oceans all on its own.

ALBERTOSAURUS **VS.** MEGALODON

UTAHRAPTOR **VS.** TITANIS

Titanis, one of the so-called terror birds, was pretty scary. It ran fast and had a wicked beak, but this angry bird was most likely a terror only to smaller birds, lizards, and rodents. It would have been no match for the fast and intelligent *Utahraptor.*

WINNER

WINNER

STRUTHIOMIMUS VS. TITANOBOA

A 40-foot (12-m) snake versus a 14-foot (4.2-m)-long dinosaur with no teeth? No contest— if *Titanoboa* could have caught *Struthiomimus*, that is. But the ostrich-like dino would have been too quick for the supersized serpent. *Titanoboa* probably wouldn't have gotten close, making *Struthiomimus* the lucky winner here.

T. REX VS. CROCODYLUS

You'd certainly shiver at the idea of *T. rex* coming back to wreak havoc on modern humans. But the 26-foot (8-m)-long *Crocodylus* really did share Earth with early hominids, and it probably used its massive jaws to chomp up a few of our early ancestors—if it didn't swallow them whole. For this reason, *Crocodylus* takes the trophy in this nightmare-inducing matchup.

WINNER

LOOK UP!
DINOSAURS LIVE ON

A ll the dinosaurs died out at the end of the Cretaceous period, right? As it turns out—no! Remember from chapter 2 that the smallest living dinosaur is the bee hummingbird? Scientists generally agree that the birds that now walk, fly, and peck among us— from emus to eagles, from peacocks to parrots—are descended from two-legged birdlike predatory dinosaurs that lived 150 million years ago during the Jurassic period.

How did they figure that? With a fossil find, of course! In the mid-19th century, scientists unearthed in Germany the bones of a prehistoric creature that was seemingly part bird, part dino: It had birdlike wings and feathers but also the toothy jaws, bony tail, feet, and large claws of a dinosaur. As you learned in chapter 5 (page 127), this groundbreaking find—*Archaeopteryx*—was a "transitional fossil": evidence that modern birds are actually a lineage of dinosaurs that survived the extinction.

The pigeon-size *Archaeopteryx* was an "avialian," among the first dinos to take flight. The first "true" birds—or "avians"— evolved about 60 million years later and have since diversified into the multitude of species flapping among us today.

BIRDS

NUMBER OF LIVING SPECIES: **10,000**

CURRENT RANGE: **WORLDWIDE**

HABITAT: **NEARLY EVERYWHERE, FROM LOW DESERTS TO TALL MOUNTAINS**

ARCHAEOPTERYX FOSSIL

SO IF BIRDS ARE
LIVING DINOSAURS,
ARE THEY ACTUALLY
REPTILES?
TECHNICALLY,
YES!

PREHISTORIC ANIMALS 197

EXTREME-AT-A-GLANCE

① WEIRDEST MOUTH

Does this creature look familiar? Not one of the first elephants on Earth but definitely one of the weirdest, *Platybelodon* had lower tusks that were oddly flat and broad. The "shovel tusker" may have used them to scoop up vegetation like soft plants and weeds from marshes between 10 and 6 million years ago.

② BIGGEST ANTLERS

Living up to about 7,700 years ago in what is now northern Europe and Asia, *Megaloceros* was one of the largest deer ever known. The males of the species sported the most immense antlers ever on a mammal—nearly 12 feet (3.7 m) from tip to tip—which were shed and regrown every year.

③ MOST LIKE A MYTHICAL SEA MONSTER

Stretching about 65 feet (20 m) long, this eel-like, primitive whale was once exhibited as a "sea serpent" by a fossil collector! *Basilosaurus* is thought to have eaten other whales when it roamed the seas between 40 and 34 million years ago, with a bite powerful enough to pierce skin, muscle, and bone.

PLATYBELODON
(PLAT-EE-BELL-OH-DON)

BASILOSAURUS
(BA-SIL-OH-SORE-US)

MEGALOCEROS
(MEG-AH-LOE-SEH-ROSS)

A WHALE OF A TALE

Much of what scientists know about *Basilosaurus* is based on fossils found in Alabama, U.S.A. It's said that remains of the early whale were once so plentiful there that 19th-century farmers used the creature's found bone fragments in the building of stone walls! *Basilosaurus* is the official state fossil of Alabama.

HOMO SAPIENS

4 SMALLEST PRIMATE

Awwww! At just two inches (5 cm) long, tiny *Eosimias* could have fit in your pocket! This furry plant- and insect-eater lived in the woodlands of Asia about 45 to 40 million years ago and was about as small as the smallest primate alive today, the pygmy mouse lemur.

5 MOST FAMOUS

Maybe the most well-recognized of all non-dino prehistoric animals, mammoths roamed the plains of Europe, Asia, Africa, and North America in herds. These mammals—including the well-known woolly mammoth—had distinctive, upward-curving tusks that they may have used to scrape away snow when feeding across their Ice Age grasslands.

6 FIRST HUMANS

You didn't think we'd forget about you, did you? The oldest known ancestor of all hominins (humans and our extinct ancestors and relatives) may go back as far as seven million years, but the first hominin almost identical to us—*Homo sapiens*—appeared in Africa 200,000 to 150,000 years ago.

EOSIMIAS
(EE-OH-SIM-EE-US)

MAMMOTH

SOME SCIENTISTS THINK **BRINGING BACK EXTINCT SPECIES** COULD HELP RESTORE DAMAGED ECOSYSTEMS.

BRING BACK THE DINOS!

(EH ... MAYBE ...)

Extinction is forever—or maybe not. Some scientists are trying to bring back long-gone animals, or at least create genetically engineered versions that are a lot like ones that have gone extinct.

How would they do that? First, they'd need some of the extinct animal's DNA. In living things, DNA is like a set of instructions; it provides the information necessary for the creation and development of plants and animals. Because the DNA of extinct animals is usually damaged and incomplete, scientists fill in the missing bits with DNA from the nearest living relatives of the animal they are trying to re-create. The resulting creation is not an exact copy of the extinct animal, but it is very similar. The plan might work for animals like the woolly mammoth and the passenger pigeon, for which intact DNA exists, but we're not likely to see a living dinosaur any time soon. Why not? Dinosaurs lived too long ago for substantial amounts of their DNA to have survived. But some scientists are trying to make chickens (the closest living relative of *T. rex*) look like dinosaurs by getting the poultry to redevelop some of the characteristics dinosaurs lost as they evolved into birds. So far they've made chicken embryos with clawed hands, wide snouts, and dinosaur ankles—fascinating for sure, but a far cry from the real thing.

DO I KNOW YOU?

Birds aren't the only animals whose relatives go back a very long way. Match the modern animal to its prehistoric ancestor.

PLATYBELODON
(PLAT-EE-BELL-OH-DON)

A

BASILOSAURUS
(BA-SIL-OH-SORE-US)

D

CERATOGAULUS
(SEH-RAT-O-GOW-LUS)

G

1. BAT

2. PYGMY MOUSE LEMUR

3. WHALE

4. ELEPHANT

5. HORSE

6. GREAT WHITE SHARK

7. SLOTH

8. RHINOCEROS

EOSIMIAS
(EE-OH-SIM-EE-US)

C

B

ICARONYCTERIS
(ICK-AH-ROE-NICK-TEH-RISS)

E

F

MERYCHIPPUS
(MEH-REE-CHIP-US)

MEGALODON
(MEG-UH-LO-DON)

H

MEGATHERIUM
(MEG-AH-THEE-REE-UM)

ANSWERS
1.B; 2.C; 3.
D; 4.A; 5.E;
6.F; 7.H; 8.G

INDEX

Boldface indicates illustrations.

ILLUSTRATION CREDITS

ACKNOWLEDGMENTS

IN MEMORY OF MY INDOMITABLE FATHER—J.A.

FOR GARTH AND WIL, WHO WORE THE (VERY UNCOMFORTABLE) *VELOCIRAPTOR* COSTUME—A.E.H.

Since 1888, the National Geographic Society has funded more than 12,000 research, exploration, and preservation projects around the world. The Society receives funds from National Geographic Partners, LLC, funded in part by your purchase. A portion of the proceeds from this book supports this vital work. To learn more, visit natgeo.com/info.

For more information, visit nationalgeographic.com, call 1-800-647-5463, or write to the following address:

National Geographic Partners
1145 17th Street N.W.
Washington, D.C. 20036-4688 U.S.A.

Visit us online at nationalgeographic.com/books

For librarians and teachers: ngchildrensbooks.org

More for kids from National Geographic:
kids.nationalgeographic.com

For information about special discounts for bulk purchases, please contact National Geographic Books Special Sales: specialsales@natgeo.com

For rights or permissions inquiries, please contact National Geographic Books Subsidiary Rights: bookrights@natgeo.com

Art directed by Callie Broaddus
Designed by Nicole Lazarus

Trade paperback ISBN: 978-1-4263-2794-0
Reinforced library binding ISBN: 978-1-4263- 2795-7

Printed in China
17/RRDS/1

The publisher and authors gratefully acknowledge the assistance and expertise of scientific adviser Nizar Ibrahim, Ph.D., paleontologist and National Geographic Explorer.

Special thanks to Franco Tempesta for creating illustrations that brought the book's prehistoric creatures to life in living color.

Thank you also to the following people for making this book possible: Becky Baines, senior editor; Ashlee Brown Blewett, project editor; Callie Broaddus, art director; Nicole Lazarus, designer; Sarah J. Mock, senior photo editor; Joan Gossett, editorial production manager; Jennifer Kelly Geddes, fact-checker; Gus Tello, design production assistant.

DRACORAPTOR